INT
ISSI
OP
VIE

C000104256

Self-Advocacy and Disability Rights

M. M. Eboch, Book Editor

GREENHAVEN
PUBLISHING

Published in 2019 by Greenhaven Publishing, LLC
353 3rd Avenue, Suite 255, New York, NY 10010

Library of Congress Cataloging-in-Publication Data

Names: Eboch, M. M., editor.
Title: Self-advocacy and disability rights / M. M. Eboch, book editor.
Description: First edition. | New York : Greenhaven Publishing, 2019. |
  Series: Introducing issues with opposing viewpoints | Includes bibliographical
  references and index. | Audience: Grades 7–12.
Identifiers: LCCN 2018028832| ISBN 9781534504257 (library bound) | ISBN
  9781534504875 (pbk.)
Subjects: LCSH: People with disabilities—Civil rights—United
  States—Juvenile literature. | Human rights advocacy—United
  States—Juvenile literature.
Classification: LCC HV1553 .S439 2019 | DDC 323.3/70973—dc23
LC record available at https://lccn.loc.gov/2018028832

Manufactured in the United States of America

Website: http://greenhavenpublishing.com

Contents

Foreword

Indulging in a wide spectrum of ideas, beliefs, and perspectives is a critical cornerstone of democracy. After all, it is often debates over differences of opinion, such as whether to legalize abortion, how to treat prisoners, or when to enact the death penalty, that shape our society and drive it forward. Such diversity of thought is frequently regarded as the hallmark of a healthy and civilized culture. As the Reverend Clifford Schutjer of the First Congregational Church in Mansfield, Ohio, declared in a 2001 sermon, "Surrounding oneself with only like-minded people, restricting what we listen to or read only to what we find agreeable is irresponsible. Refusing to entertain doubts once we make up our minds is a subtle but deadly form of arrogance." With this advice in mind, Introducing Issues with Opposing Viewpoints books aim to open readers' minds to the critically divergent views that comprise our world's most important debates.

Introducing Issues with Opposing Viewpoints simplifies for students the enormous and often overwhelming mass of material now available via print and electronic media. Collected in every volume is an array of opinions that captures the essence of a particular controversy or topic. Introducing Issues with Opposing Viewpoints books embody the spirit of nineteenth-century journalist Charles A. Dana's axiom: "Fight for your opinions, but do not believe that they contain the whole truth, or the only truth." Absorbing such contrasting opinions teaches students to analyze the strength of an argument and compare it to its opposition. From this process readers can inform and strengthen their own opinions, or be exposed to new information that will change their minds. Introducing Issues with Opposing Viewpoints is a mosaic of different voices. The authors are statesmen, pundits, academics, journalists, corporations, and ordinary people who have felt compelled to share their experiences and ideas in a public forum. Their words have been collected from newspapers, journals, books, speeches, interviews, and the Internet, the fastest growing body of opinionated material in the world.

Introducing Issues with Opposing Viewpoints shares many of the well-known features of its critically acclaimed parent series, Opposing

Viewpoints. The articles allow readers to absorb and compare divergent perspectives. Active reading questions preface each viewpoint, requiring the student to approach the material thoughtfully and carefully. Photographs, charts, and graphs supplement each article. A thorough introduction provides readers with crucial background on an issue. An annotated bibliography points the reader toward articles, books, and websites that contain additional information on the topic. An appendix of organizations to contact contains a wide variety of charities, nonprofit organizations, political groups, and private enterprises that each hold a position on the issue at hand. Finally, a comprehensive index allows readers to locate content quickly and efficiently.

Introducing Issues with Opposing Viewpoints is also significantly different from Opposing Viewpoints. As the series title implies, its presentation will help introduce students to the concept of opposing viewpoints and learn to use this material to aid in critical writing and debate. The series' four-color, accessible format makes the books attractive and inviting to readers of all levels. In addition, each viewpoint has been carefully edited to maximize a reader's understanding of the content. Short but thorough viewpoints capture the essence of an argument. A substantial, thought-provoking essay question placed at the end of each viewpoint asks the student to further investigate the issues raised in the viewpoint, compare and contrast two authors' arguments, or consider how one might go about forming an opinion on the topic at hand. Each viewpoint contains sidebars that include at-a-glance information and handy statistics. A Facts About section located in the back of the book further supplies students with relevant facts and figures.

Following in the tradition of the Opposing Viewpoints series, Greenhaven Publishing continues to provide readers with invaluable exposure to the controversial issues that shape our world. As John Stuart Mill once wrote: "The only way in which a human being can make some approach to knowing the whole of a subject is by hearing what can be said about it by persons of every variety of opinion and studying all modes in which it can be looked at by every character of mind. No wise man ever acquired his wisdom in any mode but this." It is to this principle that Introducing Issues with Opposing Viewpoints books are dedicated.

Introduction

"Effective advocacy does more than whine. Good advocacy helps to define the outcome you want to achieve."
—Mark Sweet

The summer of 2017 saw disability advocates descend on Washington, DC. Proposed legislation would make it harder to file lawsuits under the Americans with Disabilities Act (ADA). Protesters in wheelchairs chanted, "Don't take our rights away, hands off the ADA!" Some disabled protesters were arrested for "unlawfully demonstrating." That didn't stop them from protesting again and again.

They had other battles to fight under the new Trump administration. Many disabled people were not pleased with the Secretary of Education, Betsy DeVos. She repealed documents that detailed rights for students with disabilities. Officially these documents were repealed because they were "outdated, unnecessary, or ineffective." Repealing those guidelines does not change the rights granted to students. However, the guidelines clarified certain issues. It may be harder for schools and parents to enforce rules without the additional guidelines. Critics claimed the repeal would threaten the rights of vulnerable students.

Not so long ago, people with disabilities had even fewer rights and opportunities. Schools did not have special educational programs. Students with special needs might not get to go to school at all. Employers did not have to offer even the simplest accommodations to employees with special needs. That meant few people with disabilities could get jobs. Those with wheelchairs had no easy way to use public transit or enter public buildings. They might not even be able to cross the street, because most curbs did not slope down at crosswalks. The government did not provide help for people living with disabilities. If the disabled person's family didn't have the money, time, and skills to take care of them, they might end up in an institution.

Activists have been demanding rights for disabled people for a long time. The first schools for the blind and deaf were opened in the 1800s. However, laws prevented people with disabilities from marrying or moving to the United States. In many states, laws forced disabled people into institutions where they suffered abuses. People with disabilities were often sterilized so they could not have children.

A shift in society's view of disabled people began in the 1940s. Government ads encouraged businesses to "hire the handicapped." Self-help groups and wheelchair sports gave people new social and physical activities.

A pivotal moment came in 1954 when the US Supreme Court ruled in *Brown v. Board of Education of Topeka*. The court said that separate schools for black and white children were unconstitutional. This inspired the disability rights movement. Activists protested that they were excluded from mainstream schools. Still, most public schools would not accept disabled children. The Rehabilitation Act of 1973 was meant to change this. It said people with disabilities should be included in mainstream institutions. However, its language was vague, and few government agencies complied.

People with disabilities got tired of being ignored. In 1977, groups across America joined a protest. They picketed the regional offices of the Department of Health, Education, and Welfare (HEW). They demanded that the HEW Secretary sign binding regulations. These rules would guide agencies in following the Rehabilitation Act.

Most protests ended that day, but not in San Francisco. There, over 100 protesters took over the local office and stayed for about 26 days. Outside, even more protesters held daily rallies to keep the public and media's attention. Representatives then went to Washington, DC. Finally, the HEW Secretary signed the regulations. Nondiscrimination became a legal, basic right. Government buildings installed ramps and wider restroom stalls. Workplaces, university classrooms, and public buildings made changes.

In the following decades, more laws passed to protect the rights of people with disabilities. Often it took years of protest and activism to create change. The Education for All Handicapped Children Act passed in 1975. It established the right of children with disabilities to a public school education. Later, the act was renamed the Individuals with Disabilities Education Act (IDEA).

The Americans with Disabilities Act (ADA) passed in 1990. It prohibits discrimination against people with disabilities. Its rules cover jobs, schools, transportation, and all places that are open to the general public. Its goal is powerful: to make sure that people with disabilities have the same rights and opportunities as everyone else.

Yet people with disabilities still struggle in many ways. Less than 20 percent hold down jobs, and of those who do, more than a third only work part-time. Many people who have disabilities could join the workforce. However, they might need special accommodations on the job. Some companies recognize the benefits of a diverse workforce that includes people with disabilities. Other companies find it easier to avoid hiring anyone with special needs. People with disabilities may also struggle to get to a job. Some may not be able to drive, or they may have trouble with wheelchairs or crutches in bad weather.

Healthcare is another challenge. The government may provide disability benefits to people with long-term medical conditions. Often these benefits are better than the health care someone could receive from a job. That means someone may have to avoid working in order to receive the healthcare they need. Even with disability benefits, people may struggle to get the proper care and find a way to pay for it.

Opportunities have improved for people with disabilities. Yet some disability advocates are afraid that the country is going backward. The ADA Education and Reform Act (HR 620) passed the House of Representatives in 2018. As of this writing, it has not yet passed the Senate. Most disability advocates oppose this bill. They claim it weakens civil rights and makes it easier for businesses to discriminate.

As the recent attacks on disability rights show, the battle for equal rights is not over. The protests and court challenges will continue. Meanwhile, individuals will struggle to get their own needs met. People with disabilities need to know how to advocate for their needs. They also need to know when and how to get professional help. This issue is explored in *Introducing Issues with Opposing Viewpoints: Self-Advocacy and Disability Rights*, shedding light on this ongoing contemporary issue.

Chapter 1

What Special Challenges Do People with Disabilities Face?

People with disabilities face more challenges every day than we can imagine.

Integrated Classrooms Benefit Everyone

Michelle Liew

"All students grow when schools include special needs children in a mainstream environment."

In the following viewpoint, Michelle Liew argues that children with special needs should be integrated into mainstream schools. In education, integration refers to including students with special needs in regular classrooms, rather than placing them in special education classes. The author notes that integration may lead to special challenges, yet she claims that the results are worthwhile. She discusses benefits for both special needs children and their classmates. These include both educational benefits and opportunities for socialization and making friends. However, the author notes that children must be judged as individuals to determine when they are ready for mainstream classes. In order to successfully integrate special needs students, schools need teachers with proper training. Additional support staff can also help. Michelle Liew is a professional freelance writer.

"Is Integrating Children with Special Needs in Mainstream Classrooms Beneficial?" by Michelle Liew Tsui-Lin, Michelle Liew, November 10, 2016. Reprinted by permission.

AS YOU READ, CONSIDER THE FOLLOWING QUESTIONS:

1. What are the benefits of including students with reading difficulties in a mainstream classroom, according to the author?
2. How does integration benefit social skills, according to the
   viewpoint?
3. How can students who do not have special needs benefit from
   having special needs classmates, according to the author?

E very person is born with a purpose and the ability to give to
society in one way or another. It is inevitable that some may
have more needs than others. Integrating children with special needs into mainstream schools, unarguably, promotes a more
inclusive society. That said, this integration brings with it situations
that need addressing. Administrators should consider them when
including these children in a mainstream classroom.

One of my teaching assignments was in a school for children
with hearing challenges. Some of them had traces of autism. The
experience taught me that integrating children with special needs is
not without challenges. Yet, such inclusion is very important for developing an empathetic, well-rounded society. It is vital to nurture
children with special needs, for they are society's future contributing
members.

Integrating these children into a mainstream classroom has count-
less benefits. They extend to both themselves and others without these
needs. There are factors for administrators to consider if integration
into the mainstream classroom environment becomes an option.

What It Is Like Teaching Children
with Hearing Challenges

Some years ago, I left teaching in a secondary school and went instead
to teach students who had impaired hearing. Breaking down mathematical concepts into manageable processes was a daily, interesting
and fruitful challenge. So was teaching them to read, which I did
with simple sentences, word structures and catchy songs. Sorting out
mathematical concepts with manipulates and cards was challenging

Including students with impairments and disabilities in a traditional classroom is called mainstreaming.

as well. The efforts bore fruit when some children began to read with more facility. Increasingly, they used manipulates to complete problem sums.

What made this school worthy of mention was that it made some genuine, though not always successful, attempts at including students with hearing impairment in a mainstream classroom. Teachers, including myself, had to wear FM transmitters so that they could properly communicate with students who had difficulties hearing. They attended classes in a mainstream setting with students with normal hearing. What was significant was that students with hearing difficulties learned positive social communication, while their peers without such difficulties learned to empathize with the obstacles they had to face.

Teaching Students with a Mild Level of Autism

Not too long ago, a student with mild autism attended one of my classes. He spoke well, but had difficulties connecting with literature as a subject. Socially, he coped admirably. He may have had some disagreements with his peers from mainstream environments, but they came to accept his differences and difficulties. He made many friends.

This boy even learned to play the piano. I had him over to my house several times and helped him compose a tune based on his favorite animated film. With such opportunities and support from his parents, we saw a distinct improvement in his grades.

What Are the Benefits of Integration for the Special Needs Child

More than 15 years of research has proven the benefits of inclusion for all involved in the process. All students grow when schools include special needs children in a mainstream environment.

Greater Access to the Mainstream Curriculum

Students with special needs have more opportunities for academic growth because they have greater access to the mainstream curriculum. With greater exposure to the challenges of learning, they have better chances to take bigger steps forward.

In the above school for children with hearing challenges, students with both reduced hearing levels and Asperger's Syndrome benefited greatly from integration in the mainstream curriculum, achieving outstanding results. They went on to do very well in various secondary schools.

Improved Reading Levels

Children with special needs, and hence, reading difficulties, benefit greatly from inclusion in the mainstream. The reading levels of their mainstream peers also increase.

Before entering a mainstream environment, a student who had impaired hearing and difficulties with speech did not have good diction when pronouncing some of his words. He amazed me a few months later by speaking with increased fluency and better pronunciation. He claimed that he learned to say certain words from listening to a friend sitting next to him.

Increased Social Opportunities and Exposure to Proper Role Models

Integration into the mainstream for the child with special needs means the chance to interact with peers from mainstream environments. Such play is a way of developing proper socialization skills for any child, and is indispensable. The role modeling helps to nurture social skills.

Increased Skill Acquisition Opportunities

The mainstream curriculum presents the special needs child with more chances to acquire the skills that are not necessarily included in a special needs curriculum. For instance, more mathematical concepts would be included in a mainstream curriculum than in one targeted at children with more needs.

Increased Parental Participation

Parents whose children have special needs are often motivated to volunteer in their child's school community and their child's needs.

The mother of the autistic boy in my literature class was always present for Parent Teacher Conferences and volunteering to help in school based activities. This was beneficial for both her and her child, as she had greater awareness of how the school operated. She was better able to help her child at home as well.

Greater Opportunities to Be Integrated Into the Community

Being in a mainstream environment affords more opportunity for children to be able to socialize This creates a higher chance of acceptance into the community.

Many children with special needs in the mainstream school where I taught made many friends and were widely accepted by them. More often than not, children in the mainstream environment accept them once their needs are explained.

Increased Self Respect and Confidence

Being in a mainstream environment creates more self-respect and confidence for a child with special needs. Their self-esteem is given a great boost when they are around their peers in the mainstream environment.

Preparation for Adult Life in an Inclusive Society

Having the same experiences as their peers in a mainstream environment means that children with special needs are prepared for the rigors of adult life. They are armed with the sets of social and emotional skills necessary for coping with adult life.

Higher Employment Rate Among Those with Special Needs

If children with special needs have the same sets of skills developed as their peers in mainstream schools, they are also better prepared to be contributing members of the workforce.

Does Integrating Children with Special Needs Have Benefits?

Students without special needs will benefit from having their friends with those needs included in the environment as well.

Increased Application of Strategies Beneficial to All Students

The teacher in an inclusive classroom has to use strategies that will help children who progress, academically, at different rates. The all rounded approach will benefit both students with and without special needs.

Enhanced Feelings of Self-esteem

Students without special needs can experience feelings of self-esteem when asked to help or tutor their disadvantaged peers. I paired a female student with the boy with autism I mentioned earlier. She was never respected by her classmates, for she was reserved and quiet. Pairing her with the boy helped her feel better about herself, her ability to understand literature and allowed her to help him as well.

Empathy for the Limitations of Others

When students without special needs see their peers with these needs on a regular basis, there is a higher potential for developing sensitivity and empathy for their limitations. They will know why they learn at a slower pace.

The students in the class the boy with autism belonged to were initially rather apprehensive when they saw him lose his temper over trivial matters. The form teacher's explanation of his needs and how to relate to him helped tremendously with the integration.

Preparation for Integration in an Inclusive Society

Students without special needs will come to accept that those with these needs can make contributions to society. They will build better rapport with others and understand their difficulties better when they enter the workforce.

What Do Administrators Have to Consider When Integrating Children with Special Needs into Mainstream Schools?

Integrating children with special needs in a regular, mainstream classroom comes with issues that need addressing. Awareness of these issues enables successful integration.

Properly Trained Teaching Staff

One of the difficulties of including special needs children in mainstream classes is that the teacher in charge of the class might not have formal training in special education. To enable him or her to empathize with and handle its difficulties, such training is necessary.

Support Staff

Mainstream schools should have available support staff to help a special needs child with any difficulties he may have. It is a task for a teacher, who is addressing the problems that come with mainstream teaching, to balance this with the demands of teaching a child with special needs.

Schools which have decided to include children with special needs into their environment must have properly trained support staff.

The Child's Readiness

It is not wise to integrate a child into a mainstream classroom when he is not developmentally ready. This applies academically, emotionally and mentally. There are physical difficulties involved in integration, so a school should do so only after it has assessed the child's readiness level.

Breaks/Recess/Lunch

Children with special needs have a higher tendency to find themselves in difficult situations during breaks, when they are not supervised. They may get lost or into unintended altercations with other children. Children who display traces of autism may also find it difficult to shut out lunch time noises.

The best way to counter theses problems is to occupy them during these breaks. The boy with autism in my literature class often came to me during recess for piano lessons. He kept himself gainfully busy.

Changing Classrooms Between Subjects

This is the time when a child with special needs might become lost. It likely happens when he is first introduced to a new environment. A way of countering this potential problem is to assign a buddy who can help to guide the child to the correct room.

Writing Assignments

Children with special needs will need more time to complete written assignments. This is especially true of language assignments or testing situations.

A few students with special needs in the mainstream school where I taught were given an added half an hour to complete their tests and assignments. One or two actually surpassed their mainstream peers in terms of academic performance.

Punishment

Teachers need to develop alternative ways to manage special needs students who are a little restless in the classroom. They need to know how to react when these students lose control of their emotions.

What I did with special needs children in my classroom was to constantly reinforce that certain behaviors were not socially acceptable. That said, it is important not to punish children for behaviors that they cannot control. An example of this is talking too loudly. To ease these difficulties, parents should communicate them to teachers.

Conclusion

Including special needs children in a mainstream classroom benefits all students socially, emotionally and academically. It comes with challenges, but patience and effort makes it a fulfilling process.

> **EVALUATING THE AUTHOR'S ARGUMENTS:**
>
> In this viewpoint, Michelle Liew claims that including special needs students in mainstream classrooms is beneficial despite its challenges. Do the benefits she notes seem to outweigh the challenges she describes?

Finding Jobs Is Hard for People with Disabilities

Ann Belser

"The odds are long that as a man with a disability—he uses a manual wheelchair— he could find a job at all."

In the following viewpoint Ann Belser spotlights the challenges disabled people have in finding jobs. People with disabilities have much higher rates of unemployment and are more likely to work part-time than full-time. One major problem is health insurance. People with expensive health needs may be better off claiming disability benefits rather than working a job that won't pay for their healthcare. Disability benefits are government payments made to people with long-term medical conditions that prevent them from working. People with disabilities may face additional challenges, such as difficulty getting to a job site. Yet including them in the workforce is good for both the people with disabilities, and for employers, according to the article. Belser is a former reporter for the *Pittsburgh Post-Gazette*.

AS YOU READ, CONSIDER THE FOLLOWING QUESTIONS:

1. What percent of people with disabilities are in the labor force?
2. What benefits can people with disabilities bring to a job, according to the viewpoint?
3. Why is health insurance an issue for disabled people seeking work?

People with physical disabilities are at a disadvantage in the workforce. But these individuals can bring an important perspective and dedication to companies that hire them.

Chaz Kellem beat the odds.

A graduate of City Charter High School, Downtown, Mr. Kellem went to Edinboro University of Pennsylvania where he studied sports administration, hoping to land a job with a major league team. Despite intense competition in his field, the 27-year-old is now working full time for the Pittsburgh Pirates as their manager of diversity initiatives.

"I'm very lucky and blessed," he said.

Mr. Kellem is more lucky than he knows. The odds are long that as a man with a disability—he uses a manual wheelchair—he could find a job at all.

Less than one in five people with disabilities (19.2 percent) are even in the labor force, according to a first-ever study of the labor force characteristics of people with disabilities by the Bureau of Labor Statistics released this month. For people without disabilities, the labor force participation rate is 64.5 percent.

And, while it is always extra challenging to get a job if someone has a disability, this recession has been particularly unkind. In 2009, when the annual unemployment rate for people without disabilities was 9 percent, the rate for people who have disabilities was 14.5 percent.

For people with disabilities, finding a job is hard and finding a full-time job is harder. The bureau found that a full third of the people with disabilities were working part time, while just a fifth of people who are not disabled work part time.

The bureau's findings didn't surprise anyone involved in the community of people with disabilities.

Part of the problem in achieving higher employment levels in the disabled community goes right to a problem that has plagued the entire nation: health insurance.

"They are stuck in this disability benefit world," said Andrew J. Imparato, the president and CEO of the American Association of People with Disabilities in Washington, D.C.

He explained that the disabled community was hardly a monolith—instead it encompasses a huge population of people with physical, developmental and psychiatric disabilities. Their needs are as varied as they are.

However, in many cases, particularly for people with physical disabilities, their cost for health care exceeds what they could earn at a job. And many jobs don't provide the level of health benefits a person with a disability could receive through Medicare or Medicaid.

"We need to establish as a national policy that you are not going to be worse off because you took a job," Mr. Imparato said.

"We're always fighting the system. Whether it is SSI [Supplemental Security Income] or SSDI [Social Security Disability Insurance], we're stuck," said Josie Badger, 26, of Ross.

Ms. Badger has muscular dystrophy. She uses a powered wheelchair, breathes with the assistance of a ventilator and has a service dog and attendants who help with her daily routine. She is studying for a doctorate in health care ethics at Duquesne University and works part time for the Allegheny County Health Department. She already has a master's degree in rehabilitation counseling from the University of Pittsburgh.

If she took a full-time job or got married, she would lose the health insurance benefits she receives through her parents' insurer.

If it weren't for the issue of health insurance, she said, more employers would open their doors to workers with disabilities.

"It's not the employers; it's the red tape that's keeping people with disabilities from getting jobs," she said.

Mr. Imparato and Ms. Badger agreed people with disabilities bring experiences to industry that other people do not. Mr. Imparato, who has bipolar disorder, said job seekers should be upfront about their disability and what it can bring to their employment in terms of experience.

Rachel Kallem, 25, of Greenfield, calls it "disability pride."

She said she now knows not to walk into a job interview and announce that she has bipolar disorder and attention deficit hyperactivity disorder, but she doesn't shy away from it either.

Some companies have developed a reputation for a commitment to the employment of people with disabilities, including Highmark and Bayer Corp.

Bayer has created a one-year jobs program in which people with disabilities gain experience and feedback while Bayer gets workers whom the company has found to be extremely dedicated to the corporation.

Bryan Iams, a spokesman for the company, said Bayer started the program, in part, to fill a need in the information technology division of the corporation where there is a high turnover rate. Now it has expanded to other areas.

People in the program "bring that level of dedication and commitment and interest that you really can't easily find; and when we do find it, it's really valuable to the team and the company," he said.

But people with disabilities face challenges that others may not even consider.

For Steve Kohut, 44, of Brentwood, part of the impediment to finding a job is being sure he will be able to make the commute in bad weather.

Mr. Kohut has muscular dystrophy and stopped working eight years ago after a series of falls.

"After the falls, I had to move home with my mom and dad," he said.

Now he has a battery-powered wheelchair, but he is not sure he will be able to make it across the back lawn when it gets too snowy or muddy to get to the car.

Mr. Kellem has similar problems. He needs help moving boxes for work and has to take extra time in the snow. But he said in the community affairs department of the Pittsburgh Pirates where he landed against so many odds, he has found not just a job but a supportive home.

EVALUATING THE AUTHOR'S ARGUMENTS:

Viewpoint author Ann Belser argues that people with disabilities bring special benefits to their employers. Yet they may also need special accommodations. How might an employer judge these factors? Should a person's disabilities play a part in whether or not they are hired for a job? Why or why not?

Viewpoint

3

Travel Is a Challenge for Those with Disabilities

John Gill

> "The principle of equal treatment is particularly relevant to the public transport sector."

In the following viewpoint, John Gill discusses some of the problems people with disabilities may have in traveling. Statistics from interviews support the claims that people with disabilities may have trouble with various forms of transportation. The author then gives some examples to explain why poorly designed facilities can cause problems. Businesses should improve the accessibility of their services, according to the author. Several reasons are given, including the growing population of the elderly and people with disabilities. The author also notes that customers without disabilities would benefit from easier and more convenient public transportation. John Gill is an accessibility of information technology consultant.

AS YOU READ, CONSIDER THE FOLLOWING QUESTIONS:

1. Why do disabled people use taxis more often than public transport such as buses, according to the viewpoint?
2. What challenges do people with vision difficulties face when it comes to public transportation?
3. Why are stairs a problem for some people with physical impairments?

"Difficulties Disabled Passengers Face with Public Transport," John Gill Technology. Reprinted by permission.

Just getting to school or work each day can be a trial for those with physical disabilities. The challenges often discourage mobility and can result in isolation.

Be it trains, planes or automobiles disabled people still face massive challenges in getting around.

- Disabled people travel a third less often than other people
- Over a third of disabled people who do travel experience difficulties, the most common being getting on or off trains or buses
- The national average for accessibility of buses is only around 30%
- Of disabled people who use public transport, over half (56%) have to resort to using costly taxis for easier access
- Nearly two-thirds (60%) of households containing a disabled person do not have access to a private car, compared to 27% of the general population
- More than one in five spaces reserved for disabled drivers are abused by non-disabled motorists

- In terms of convenience and ease of use, taxis and minicabs are rated the most highly, with rail services the worst
- Eight in ten disabled people never use light rail, tram or Underground services. Three-quarters never use ferry services and two-thirds do not fly
- Bus drivers are rated as the most unhelpful public transport employees by disabled people, with 20% of respondents saying that they are unhelpful, compared with 13% for train station staff, 6% for both on train staff and taxi drivers, and just 2% for airline stewards
- Nearly half (41%) of disabled people in England and Wales say they experience difficulty with traveling. A quarter (25%) experience difficulty travelling to and from the doctor or hospital, 23% have experienced problems visiting friends or relatives and 18% visiting leisure facilities. Some 23% of disabled workers say they find travelling to and from their place of work difficult

The Department for Works and Pensions (DWP) Disabled for Life research found that the difficulties most commonly mentioned by disabled people in Great Britain were getting to and from bus stops or stations (22%) or on and off buses and trains (24%).

Blind and partially sighted passengers may find it difficult in using stairs. Particularly if the design of handrails and the appropriate use of tactile warnings and colour contrast have not been considered. Visual information with no audible backup might present blind and partially sighted passengers with serious difficulty. Poor quality audible information will be a problem for blind and partially sighted passengers who rely solely on audible information. Glare from the glass screen at a ticket counter will be a problem because it makes use of their residual vision more difficult.

Lack of visual information is a problem to passengers who are deaf or hard of hearing. Glare from the glass screen at a ticket counter is a problem for passengers who are deaf or hard of hearing because they

Difficulties experienced by disabled people

Type of difficulty	Percentage
Getting to rail/bus station/stop	13%
Getting into rail/bus station	10%
Getting on/off bus or train	24%
Travelling by taxi	8%
Changing modes of transport	8%
Getting from bus stop/train station	9%
Getting information about accessible transport	6%
Booking tickets	4%
Ensuring assistance is available	5%
Other difficulties	2%
Same as non-disabled people	7%
No difficulties	57%

The above information was obtained from Disablist Britain—Barriers to Independent Living for Disabled People in 2006. Paul Miller, Sarah Gillinson and Julia Huber, Demos

cannot see the other person's face for visual clues or lip-reading. Poor quality audible information is also a problem for passengers who are hard of hearing, especially where there is significant background noise.

A flight of stairs is a problem to a physically impaired passenger (ie. a wheelchair user) and to an elderly passenger. A confusing station layout is a problem for someone with walking difficulties and an elderly passenger, who may in consequence have to walk farther.

Cognitively impaired passengers would find a lack of visual information a problem. Poor signage, especially signage without appropriate pictograms, is a problem for cognitively impaired passengers.

They would also have a problem with a confusing station layout as they may lose their way.

There are a number of reasons why operators should improve the accessibility of their services.

Firstly, improving accessibility is good for business. The profile of passengers (and potential passengers) of public transport is changing. Not only is the number of people with disabilities growing but the proportion of older people in the population is also increasing. These demographic changes will require improvement in the accessibility of public transport services. Improving accessibility will attract passengers who would not previously have considered using public transport.

Existing passengers, who may or may not have disabilities, will be encouraged to make more trips by public transport because it is easier or more convenient to use, more pleasant and satisfies their needs to a fuller extent. The introduction of low floor, accessible vehicles may also lead to reduction in dwell times at stops and stations as passengers can get on and off low floor vehicles more easily and quicker, thereby enabling vehicles to complete journeys quicker and thus possibly reducing the number of vehicles required to provide the same level of service.

Secondly, the legislative and regulatory framework has become more demanding for all parties in relation to providing fully accessible public transport services.

Finally, all citizens should be given equal consideration in the design and provision of public transport. The principle of equal treatment is particularly relevant to the public transport sector as it has the ability to enable people to gain access to all that society has to offer.

EVALUATING THE AUTHOR'S ARGUMENTS:

In this viewpoint, John Gill suggests businesses should improve the accessibility of their services. Are clear, logical reasons given to support the argument? If you were a business owner, would you be convinced? Why or why not?

This New Law Could Hurt People with Disabilities

Robyn Powell

"Despite its name, disability advocates believe this bill is an assault on their civil rights and will weaken protections afforded to them under the ADA."

In the following viewpoint, Robyn Powell describes a 2018 bill that she says will harm people with disabilities. In response to the bill, activists protested at the US Capitol. Still, the bill passed in the House of Representatives, supported primarily by Republican politicians. At the time of this writing, the bill had not been passed by the Senate. The author quotes several people who describe the bill as a blow against civil rights. Civil rights are the rights of citizens to political and social freedom and equality. A range of civil rights are guaranteed by the US Constitution and laws. Robyn Powell works in the field of disability law and policy and is an authority on the rights of parents with disabilities. Powell is an attorney and researcher at the Lurie Institute for Disability Policy at Brandeis University.

"When Fear Turned into Fact: Congress' Move to Gut the Americans with Disabilities Act Spurs Protests," by Robyn Powell, Rewire News, February 12, 2018. Published with permission from Rewire.News. https://rewire.news/article/2018/02/22/fear-fact-congress-move-to-gut-the-americans-with-disabilities-act-spurs-protests/.

AS YOU READ, CONSIDER THE FOLLOWING QUESTIONS:
1. What do people in favor of HR 620 claim as its benefits?
2. What do people against HR 620 claim as its problems?
3. How is a bill that affects people with disabilities a civil rights issue?

Last week, the US House of Representatives passed the ADA Education and Reform Act (HR 620). Despite its name, disability advocates believe this bill is an assault on their civil rights and will weaken protections afforded to them under the Americans with Disabilities Act (ADA).

The 225-192 vote was primarily along party lines, with only 19 Republicans opposed to the bill. Twelve Democrats voted in support, including six from California—Reps. Pete Aguilar, Ami Bera, Lou Correa, Scott Peters, Jackie Speier, and Norma Torres—as well as Reps. Jim Cooper (TN), Henry Cuellar (TX), Bill Foster (IL), Collin Peterson (MN), Kathleen Rice (NY), and Kurt Schrader (OR).

In a final attempt to stop passage of the bill, members of ADAPT, a national grassroots group that organizes disability rights activists to engage in nonviolent direct action, descended on the US Capitol. Activists filled first the House Rules Committee session, and then the House Gallery days later for the final floor vote, chanting, "Don't take our rights away; hands off the ADA."

Colleen Flanagan, co-founder and executive director of Disability Action for America and a National ADAPT organizer, was among those who were arrested twice during last week's actions. "I saw House members from the floor turn their heads toward our chanting. I remember seeing one member of Congress' jaw actually drop while he gawked at us with his mouth wide open," Flanagan, who streamed the arrests live on Twitter from the House Gallery, told Rewire via email.

"Soon the US Capitol Police flooded in the ADA-accessible viewing area where we were protesting. Cops began pushing ADAPTers in locked wheelchairs out of the viewing section," Flanagan explained, referring to wheelchairs with the brakes on.

Disability rights advocates attend a hearing regarding disability rights on Capitol Hill.

"For those in wheelchairs they couldn't push out, Capitol Police decided to literally pick up our disabled bodies and carry us out instead," Flanagan continued.

"That's how I left the House Galley ADA-accessible viewing area on Thursday," Flanagan concluded, "being carried out by a cop."

As I have explained previously for Rewire, HR 620 completely upends how the ADA is enforced. Since the law was passed nearly 28 years ago, people with disabilities have had two mechanisms for enforcing their rights if a business is inaccessible: They can file a complaint with the US Department of Justice (DOJ), which will investigate the alleged access violation and decide if a business has violated the ADA. The agency then may enter into mediation with the aggrieved individual and the business, or sue the business on the person's behalf. Otherwise, people with disabilities may file a lawsuit in court, bypassing the DOJ entirely. Typically, both enforcement mechanisms allow for swift action to resolve the violation.

However, HR 620 would require people with disabilities to give a business owner "specific enough" written notice about the accessibility violation. The business owner then would have 60 days to acknowledge the problem and another 120 days to make "substantial progress" toward resolving the access violation. Effectively, the bill would require people with disabilities to wait 180 days before they could enforce their civil rights by filing a lawsuit.

Proponents of HR 620 contend that the bill is necessary to prevent frivolous lawsuits. They believe people with disabilities and their attorneys intentionally seek out accessibility violations at businesses so that they can sue and make money.

However, HR 620 will do nothing to stop attorneys who bring frivolous lawsuits for money because the ADA does not allow courts to award monetary damages to plaintiffs. Settlements or court orders that grant money damages for accessibility violations are not based on the ADA, but rather on laws in a handful of states—including in California, whose Business Properties Association issued a statement celebrating all 14 Republicans and the six Democrats who voted "yes." Moreover, attorneys are ethically and legally not allowed to represent individuals in frivolous lawsuits. Hence, this is an issue that state courts and bar associations must address, not Congress.

Disability advocates, who believe that this bill only serves to incentivize non-compliance by businesses, have fought similar legislation for years. However, this is the first time this type of bill has made it as far along in the legislative process, and that is alarming.

In September 2017, the Consortium for Citizens with Disabilities, along with over 200 disability and civil rights organizations, issued a letter to the House Judiciary Committee strongly opposing the bill: "We know of no other law that outlaws discrimination but permits entities to discriminate with impunity until victims experience that discrimination and educate the entities perpetrating it about their obligations not to discriminate. Such a regime is absurd, and would make people with disabilities second-class citizens."

Activists were not alone in voicing their opposition to HR 620. Immediately following the House Rules Committee's vote to send the bill to the floor for a final vote, Sen. Tammy Duckworth (D-IL), issued a statement, saying, in part, "This offensive legislation would undermine civil rights in our nation and reward businesses that fail to comply with the Americans with Disabilities Act, which has been the law of the land for nearly 30 years. Passing it would send a disgraceful message to Americans with disabilities: their civil rights are not worthy of strong enforcement and they can, once again, be treated like second-class citizens." For Duckworth, who is a disabled veteran and wheelchair user, access to public accommodations is personal.

Several Democrats also expressed their concerns during the floor debate that HR 620 would roll back protections for people with disabilities. These lawmakers included Rep. John Lewis (D-GA) who told his colleagues in an impassioned speech that the bill "strikes a devastating blow in the fight for civil rights."

"This bill is wrong. It is mean-spirited, and it is a shame and a disgrace that we would bring it to the floor," Lewis continued.

Now that HR 620 has passed the House, it will head to the Senate, where some Democrats have already declared their opposition. Indeed, Duckworth, Sens. Bob Casey (D-PA), Chuck Schumer (D-NY), Maggie Hassan (D-NH), Elizabeth Warren (D-MA) and Chris Van Hollen (D-MD) issued a joint statement on Friday: "Advocates worked tirelessly to oppose the bill in the House and to protect the rights of people with disabilities. As a group of Senators who value the rights of people with disabilities and recognize that disability rights are civil rights, we will work with advocates to uphold the rights of people with disabilities and oppose any legislation that threatens those rights."

There is not a current version of the bill in the Senate yet, and thus far, Republican senators have remained silent on their positions. However, it is clear that disability activists are not backing down. "We need everyone to call their senator to let them know how critically important it is they reject similar legislation in the Senate," Flanagan told Rewire.

Activists also pointed out the fact that the passage of HR 620 marked yet another attack on disability rights during the Trump era. "The results of the 2016 election both outraged and terrified me," Flanagan said. "I feared the rights of disabled people would be the first to be attacked, and my fear since turned into fact."

EVALUATING THE AUTHOR'S ARGUMENTS:

In the viewpoint, the author claims that proposed changes to the Americans with Disabilities Act will lessen protections for disabled people. How does she support this viewpoint? How does quoting experts affect the strength of her argument?

Chapter 2

Who Is the Best Advocate for Someone with Disabilities?

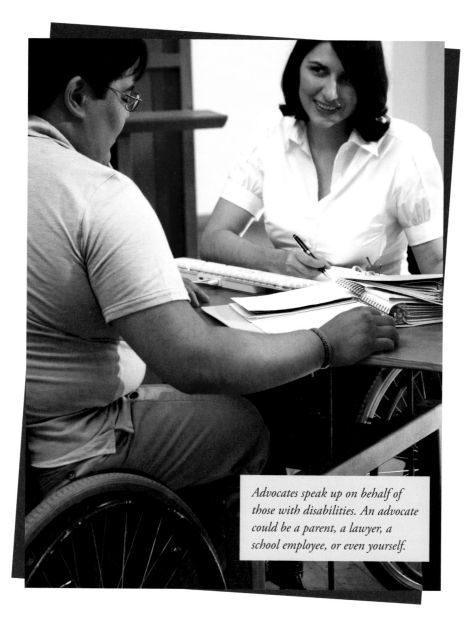

Advocates speak up on behalf of those with disabilities. An advocate could be a parent, a lawyer, a school employee, or even yourself.

Viewpoint

1

Parents Are Natural Advocates for Children with Special Needs

Peter and Pam Wright

"If you have a child with special needs, you may wind up battling the school district for the services your child needs."

In the following viewpoint, Peter and Pam Wright explain what an advocate is. Some may have specialized training, such as lay advocates, who have legal training. Advocates may also have experience in educational concerns, or they may have no special training. Next the authors describe what advocates do. They claim that parents are natural advocates for their children with special educational needs, and they give advice on how to be successful advocates. Pete Wright is an attorney who represents children with special educational needs. Pam Wright is a psychotherapist who works with children and families.

AS YOU READ, CONSIDER THE FOLLOWING QUESTIONS:
1. Why are parents natural advocates for their children?
2. Why must advocates understand legal rights?
3. Why is it important to consider the future when advocating now, according to the viewpoint?

"Advocating for Your Child," by Peter and Pam Wright, The original article can be found on site www.wrightslaw.com at the following link. http://www.wrightslaw.com/advoc/articles/advocacy.intro.htm. Reprinted by permission.

Public school students with disabilities are often assisted by aids. Often, however, parents have to act as advocates to ensure their children are given such assistance.

Good special education services are intensive and expensive. Resources are limited. If you have a child with special needs, you may wind up battling the school district for the services your child needs. To prevail, you need information, skills, and tools.

Who can be an advocate?

Anyone can advocate for another person. Here is how the dictionary defines the term "advocate": ad-vo-cate—Verb, transitive. To speak, plead or argue in favor of. Synonym is support.

1. One that argues for a cause; a supporter or defender; an advocate of civil rights.
2. One that pleads in another's behalf; an intercessor; advocates for abused children and spouses.

3. A lawyer. (The American Heritage Dictionary of the English Language, Third Edition)

An advocate performs several functions:

- Supports, helps, assists, and aids
- Speaks and pleads on behalf of others
- Defends and argues for people or causes

Different Types of Advocates

Special education advocates work to improve the lives of children with disabilities and their families. You are likely to meet different types of advocates.

Lay Advocates

Lay advocates use specialized knowledge and expertise to help parents resolve problems with schools. When lay advocates attend meetings, write letters, and negotiate for services, they are acting on the child's behalf. Most lay advocates are knowledgeable about legal rights and responsibilities. In some states, lay advocates represent parents in special education due process hearings.

Educational Advocates

Educational advocates evaluate children with disabilities and make recommendations about services, supports and special education programs. When educational advocates go to eligibility and IEP meetings, they are acting on the child's behalf. Some educational advocates negotiate for services. Others are less knowledgeable about special education law and how to use tactics and strategies.

School Personnel

Teachers and special education providers often see themselves as advocates. Teachers, administrators, and school staff often provide support to children and their families. But because they are employed by school districts, school personnel are limited in their ability to advocate for children with disabilities without endangering their jobs.

Parents

Parents are natural advocates for their children.

Who is your child's first teacher? You are. Who is your child's most important role model? You are. Who is responsible for your child's welfare? You are. Who has your child's best interests at heart? You do.

You know your child better than anyone else. The school is involved with your child for a few years. You are involved with your child for life. You should play an active role in planning your child's education.

The law gives you the power to make educational decisions for your child. Do not be afraid to use your power. Use it wisely. A good education is the most important gift you can give to your child.

As the parent of a child with a disability, you have two goals:

* To ensure that the school provides your child with a "free appropriate public education" that includes "specially designed instruction ... to meet the [child's] unique needs ..." (20 U.S.C. §1401)
* To build a healthy working relationship with the school.

What Advocates Do

Advocacy is not a mysterious process. Here is a quick overview of advocacy skills.

Gather Information

Advocates gather facts and information. As they gather information and organize documents, they learn about the child's disability and educational history. Advocates use facts and independent documentation to resolve disagreements and disputes with the school.

Learn the Rules of the Game

Advocates educate themselves about their local school district. They know how decisions are made and by whom.

Advocates know about legal rights. They know that a child with a disability is entitled to an "appropriate" education, not the "best" education, nor an education that "maximizes the child's potential."

They understand that "best" is a four-letter word that cannot be used by parents or advocates.

Advocates know the procedures that parents must follow to protect their rights and the child's rights.

Plan and Prepare

Advocates know that planning prevents problems. Advocates do not expect school personnel to tell them about rights and responsibilities. Advocates read special education laws, regulations, and cases to get answers to their questions.

Advocates learn how to use test scores to monitor a child's progress in special education. They prepare for meetings, create agendas, write objectives, and use meeting worksheets and follow-up letters to clarify problems and nail down agreements.

Keep Written Records

Because documents are often the keys to success, advocates keep written records. They know that if a statement is not written down, it was not said. They make requests in writing and write polite follow-up letters to document events, discussions, and meetings.

Ask Questions, Listen to Answers

Advocates are not afraid to ask questions. When they ask questions, they listen carefully to answers. Advocates know how to use "Who, What, Why, Where, When, How, and Explain Questions" (5 Ws + H + E) to discover the true reasons for positions.

Identify Problems

Advocates learn to define and describe problems from all angles. They use their knowledge of interests, fears, and positions to develop strategies. Advocates are problem solvers. They do not waste valuable time and energy looking for people to blame.

Propose Solutions

Advocates know that parents negotiate with schools for special education services. As negotiators, advocates discuss issues and make offers or proposals. They seek "win-win" solutions that will satisfy the interests of parents and schools.

Your Assignment
Plan for the Future

What are your long-term goals for your child? What do you envision for your child in the future? If you are like most parents, you are focused on the present. You haven't given much thought to the future.

Do you expect your child to be an independent, self-sufficient member of the community? Although some children with disabilities will require assistance as adults, most will grow up to be adults who hold jobs, get married, and live independently.

If you have a vision about what you want for your child in the future, you are more likely to achieve your goals.

If you believe others will make long-term plans for your child and provide your child with the necessary skills to be an independent, self-sufficient member of society, you are likely to be disappointed.

Answer Questions

What do you want for your child? What are your goals for your child's future? Do you have a master plan for your child's education?

If you want your child to grow up to be an independent adult, what does your child need to learn before he or she leaves the public school system?

What do you want?

Develop a Master Plan

If you are like many parents, you don't have a master plan. You don't know where you are, where you need to go, or how to get there. Do not expect school personnel to make long-term plans for your child—this is your responsibility.

Begin by thinking about your vision for your child's future. What are your long-term goals for your child? What will your child need to learn? What services and supports will your child need to meet these goals?

Are you ready to advocate? Here is a list of supplies that will help you get started:

- Two 3-ring notebooks (one for your child's file; one for information about your child's disability and educational information)
- 3-hole punch
- Highlighters
- Package of sticky notes
- #10 Envelopes
- Stamps
- Calendar
- Journal
- Contact log
- Small tape or digital recorder

In this article, you learned about lay advocates and educational advocates, and about limitations on teachers and special education staff in their ability to advocate. You learned that parents are natural advocates for their children.

You learned about basic advocacy skills—gathering and organizing information, planning and preparing, documenting, problem solving, and negotiating. You have a list of supplies to help you advocate.

You learned that you must plan for your child's future. A plan is like a roadmap. When you have a plan, you know where you are, where you need to go, and how to know when you arrive.

The Parent's Journey from Emotions to Advocacy

On your journey from emotions to advocacy, you will learn about your child's disability, educational and remedial techniques, educational progress, Individualized Education Programs (IEPs), and how to artfully advocate.

You will learn how to present your concerns and problems in writing, prepare for meetings, and search for win-win solutions. You will learn how to use your emotions as a source of energy and power, and how to focus on getting an appropriate education for your child.

EVALUATING THE AUTHORS' ARGUMENTS:

Viewpoint authors Peter and Pam Wright suggest that parents are the best advocates for their children. What reasoning do they use to explain this idea? Do they make a strong case for their views? What challenges might parents face in becoming advocates for their children?

You Are Your Own Best Advocate

University of Hertfordshire

"Having a voice of your own has the power to challenge how people with intellectual disabilities are thought about in society."

In the following viewpoint, authors from the University of Hertfordshire in the United Kingdom argue that people can be their own best advocates. Self-advocacy means having your own voice, making choices, and identifying your likes and dislikes. It means having a say in your future and sometimes being allowed to take risks. These things can build confidence and self-esteem and can even can help change society's views of people with disabilities, the authors argue. They suggest that everyone is capable of having a voice, regardless of the extent of their physical or intellectual disabilities.

AS YOU READ, CONSIDER THE FOLLOWING QUESTIONS:
1. How can people who are nonverbal have a voice, according to the viewpoint?
2. Why is the ability to take a risk a type of human right?
3. How can a lack of voice lead to discrimination against people with disabilities, according to the viewpoint?

"Self Advocacy," University of Hertfordshire. Reprinted by permission.

It is important for those who are able to learn to be their own advocates, even if they also require the assistance of others.

Self-advocacy is one of the most important ways in which people with intellectual disabilities have a voice of their own. The words of Jackie Downer, a self-advocate, encapsulate all that self-advocacy has the potential to be. Her words emphasise that having a voice of your own is immensely personal and therefore is important to different people for different reasons. Through her words, the importance of people with intellectual disabilities having a voice of their own, is emphasised.

In explaining self-advocacy, Jackie says, "Broken down it means 'speaking for yourself,' 'communicating in other ways,' but it's personal. For me it means that I can speak for myself. It means I've got a voice and even without a voice I can communicate in other ways. It means yes and no—most important—'No, I don't want tea, I want coffee, I don't want sugar'—all the things we take for granted. It means people must listen to me, I can take a risk, I can have

FAST FACT

A disability is a physical or mental condition that limits a person's senses, movements, or activities. Some people have multiple disabilities.

a relationship, that can be hard. I can think for myself, I can go to the shop with support and if I need help, people can help me ..." (Jackie Downer in Goodley 2000:81).

"Speaking for Yourself"

Self-advocacy, or having a voice of your own, is fundamental to both asserting yourself and exploring yourself. This is important because it is directly linked to building confidence and self-esteem. It is important to have the possibility of talking about your life and your experiences so that who you are can be validated by others. In this way having a voice of your own has the power to construct your identity.

"I've Got a Voice and Even without a Voice I Can Communicate in Other Ways"

It is important to emphasize that having a voice of your own does not necessarily mean having a literal voice. People who are non-verbal are able to communicate themselves, their likes and dislikes, their wants and needs, in ways other than words. For example, taking a person by the hand to show them where they want to go, pointing to pictures, symbols or photographs. This is important because self-advocacy is sometimes criticized for only being relevant to people who have mild to moderate intellectual disabilities. It is necessary to acknowledge that all people, even those with severe intellectual disabilities, can communicate and express themselves.

"It Means Yes and No"

Having a voice is important as a means by which you can communicate to others who you are, what you like, what you don't like, etc. It is important because it means you can make choices about your life and about what is important to you. As Jackie's words express, it can be about seemingly small things, like whether you take sugar in your tea, or about bigger things, like where you want to live. If you have your own voice then other people are less able to make assumptions about you and your life. This is especially important for people with intellectual disabilities who have traditionally been seen as incapable, as not having their own opinions, desires and wishes, and as being dependent on those who look after them. In this way having a voice of your own gives you power.

"People Must Listen to Me"

Self-advocacy is important because people can speak out publicly. If people have a voice of their own they can comment on the services they use, can define how they want to be known- as people with intellectual disabilities rather than "handicapped," can campaign for issues which are important to them, for example the closure of institutions or how money is spent in day services, can advise on the creation of new policies and services, etc.

"I Can Take a Risk, I Can Have a Relationship"

Self-advocacy is partly about knowing your rights as a human being. This is vitally important in a society which still discriminates against people, who have the label of intellectual disability, owning their own home, falling in love, getting married, having children and working in ordinary workplaces. If you have a voice of your own you can assert the right to take a risk, to choose again and to learn from your mistakes.

"I Can Think for Myself"

One of the most important consequences of having a voice of your own is that it has the power to challenge how people with intellectual disabilities are thought about in society. They have traditionally been seen as a group who were incapable of thought, of action, of being able to live their lives as others do. This has led to their discrimination, segregation and isolation. If this perception is challenged, then people with intellectual disabilities will be nearer to being included and treated as equals in our society.

"I Can Go to the Shop with Support and If I Need Help, People Can Help Me"

Finally, having a voice of your own is important because people with intellectual disabilities have traditionally been dependant on carers, professionals, and parents, for knowing what was best for them. If people have a voice of their own then the power relationship is significantly altered. It does not deny that people with intellectual disabilities need help and support, but emphasizes that they can define what kind of help they need, when they need it and for how long. It is thus acknowledged that all people have strengths and weaknesses and that no one individual can be either totally "capable" or "incapable."

Through Jackie's words it can be seen why it is important for people with intellectual disabilities to have a voice of their own. Having a voice is important for everyone, but for people with intellectual disabilities it is crucial due to their segregated, isolated and discriminated against, position in society.

EVALUATING THE AUTHOR'S ARGUMENTS:

This viewpoint argues that people can be their own best advocates. How does this compare with the previous viewpoint, which suggested that parents are the best advocates for children with special needs? Would the age of the young person make a difference? What about the type and degree of the person's disabilities? Who should ultimately decide what is best for an individual?

A Professional Advocate Can Help

Disability Advocacy NSW

"Individual advocates who are professionally trained can help a person with a disability or their career."

In the following viewpoint, authors from an Australian agency called Disability Advocacy NSW describe how professional disability advocates work. The authors discuss what these advocates can and cannot do in various circumstances. Such agencies are experts trained in making sure those who need help are properly represented. Disability Advocacy NSW is an agency in New South Wales, Australia. It helps people of all ages with any type of disability or mental illness get fair treatment.

AS YOU READ, CONSIDER THE FOLLOWING QUESTIONS:

1. Can a professional advocate directly offer legal help?
2. How can talking over the options help someone facing a problem related to their disability?
3. How can a professional advocate assist someone who is a victim of discrimination?

Professional advocates may work on behalf of disabled people without a voice to successfully gain access to previously prohibitive locations.

Individual advocacy is essentially the process of standing up for the rights of someone who is being treated unfairly. Disability Advocacy NSW can provide short to medium term, non-legal, issue-based advocacy support to people with disability who have serious and urgent issues.

Individual advocates who are professionally trained can help a person with a disability or their career in the following ways:

- Directly advocating on behalf of a person or providing information and advice so that a person can advocate for themselves (e.g. dealing with a landlord, support when going to court, support in dealing with the police or dealing with a legal issue by getting professional legal advice, negotiating a better deal from a government department, dealing with guardianship and financial management orders, dealing with problems at work, school, TAFE or uni etc).

- Linking a person with other relevant services (e.g. helping a person get legal advice from a solicitor).
- Talking over a problem (e.g. advocate can best help by simply listening and helping to think through options for moving forward).
- Supporting an individual to take formal action on

matters related to disability discrimination or making a complaint against a service provider (e.g. assisting a person to make a complaint with the Anti-Discrimination Board).

However, please note that advocates are not able to:

- Provide case work or case management services (e.g. finding accommodation, applying for services, managing services, etc).
- Provide advocacy services when a disability support worker/case worker can provide advocacy support and they do not have a conflict of interest.
- Provide advocacy for a person when a more appropriate service is available to advocate and assist.
- Provide advocacy for a person who wishes to take out a personal violence order at court against a neighbour or workmate etc if mediation has not been attempted to resolve the dispute.

Examples of How a Disability Advocate Can Assist People with a Disability

- Accommodation (Housing) e.g. assist client with tenancy issues, negotiate for more appropriate accommodation for young people in nursing homes
- Access (Physical access) e.g. assist a client to seek improved access to a building, on behalf of clients work with local council to improve physical access to existing facilities

- Children (Custody and child protection matters) e.g. support parents with an intellectual disability in care proceedings.
- Compensation & Insurance (Accidents and injury) e.g. independently assist client to claim insurance from an accident or deal with compensation payout.
- Consumers & Contracts (Consumer protection) e.g. assist a client unfairly treated in product purchase.
- Decision making e.g. support a client at a guardianship tribunal hearing, help client to consider and understand all options in a major decision.
- Disputes e.g. assist a client to participate in and understand a dispute resolution procedure.
- Discrimination e.g. assist a client to take a disability discrimination complaint to the Australian Human Rights Commission or the Anti-Discrimination Board of NSW.
- Education e.g. assist a client who may have been excluded from a training course, assist a carer to negotiate with a school about improving the support for a child with a disability.
- Employment e.g. assist a client in dispute with work place.
- Equipment e.g. assist client who has been unfairly treated by equipment supply service.
- Finances (Debt, credit, pensions, benefits, superannuation) e.g. assist a client to challenge a pension debt.
- Health (Health consumer rights) e.g. assist client to question a medical decision or raise a complaint about treatment for a mental illness
- Offences & infringements (Crime, sexual and drug offences, traffic offences) e.g. assist a client to deal with a charge of parking infringement or assault.
- Relationships (Marriage, divorce, de facto relationships, parenting, adoption, domestic violence) e.g. assist a client to participate in family court mediation.
- Services (Disability) (Specialist disability service providers) e.g. assist a client to raise a complaint with a day program, or assist a client to access Home Care services.

- Transport e.g. assist a client unable to get access to disabled taxis.
- Wills & estates e.g. assist a carer to get advice and support to provide for client in the future or assist client to challenge a will.

EVALUATING THE AUTHOR'S ARGUMENTS:

In this viewpoint, an agency describes how a professional advocate might help someone with a disability. What is the tone of the article? Is it trying to convince the reader to take a certain action? Compare this to the previous viewpoints that discussed parent advocates and self-advocacy. Does one option seem better than the other? When might someone turn to a professional advocate for additional support?

Viewpoint 4

Parents Are the Best Advocates for Their Children

Buffy Wicks

"We are failing our children, and it is time for us to stand up and demand change from our elected officials."

In the following viewpoint, Buffy Wicks describes growing up in a working-class family. She notes that she achieved success, but few of her classmates did. She credits her achievements to her parents and suggests that parents are their children's best advocates. She calls for the state of California to do better for children and describes some of the priorities of the California Kids Campaign. Buffy Wicks is the campaign director for the California Kids Campaign, a resource for training parents to advocate for change in their own communities.

AS YOU READ, CONSIDER THE FOLLOWING QUESTIONS:

1. Roughly what percentage of children in California live in or near poverty?
2. Do communities of color have better or worse opportunities for healthy child development than predominantly White communities, according to the viewpoint?
3. What public programs could help support working families, as described by the author?

"Parents Are Their Children's Best Advocates," by Buffy Wicks, Common Sense, March 23, 2016. Reprinted by permission.

For very young children, who aren't aware of their needs or potential, parents must take on the role of advocate.

I grew up in a mobile home in a little town of 1,500 people called Foresthill, California. It's not a place you would happen across. The main road from Auburn narrows to two lanes just past the commercial drag, and the booms that brought gold and timber wealth to the area are relics of the last two centuries, respectively. Today, the town is a sleepy, ex-ex-urban community of Sacramento, with stunning views of the nearby Sierra Nevada mountains but no real economic base.

Early in my childhood, we lived in a trailer park in town, but when I was 9 my parents bought a piece of land nearby, so we towed the mobile home over to the new lot. My dad built a barn, but the mobile home was still, well, home. Lots of kids dream of having an in-ground pool. I wanted what I called a "real house," with a flight of stairs—a wooden flight of stairs that I could run up and down, that creaked and groaned and warped.

My family was squarely working class. When I was a kid, my mom didn't have an outside job. But she later attended community college and Sacramento State University, and—over the course of years—became the first person in her family to earn a college degree. My dad worked as a firefighter for the US Forest Service. They were both ascendant and, as part of a narrative so familiar to Americans in California and beyond, determined to pass the baton to their kids.

My parents raised my brother and me to work hard and think big. Internalizing such values, they reasoned, would open the world to us. They channeled my energy into sports and school activities. My mom drove me hours every day to the year-round swim team outside of Sacramento, because the local seasonal teams were too limited, and she defended my prerogatives in school when my passion for various causes raised the eyebrows of some teachers and administrators. Just as important, my parents didn't let my brother and me confine our imaginations to the experiences of small-town California. They encouraged us to follow our passion, keeping us engaged in activities that enriched our minds, saving to send me on a Close Up trip to Washington, D.C., my senior year of high school and encouraging my involvement in politics and grassroots community-based organizing.

I was a handful as a child—to say the least—but instead of throwing their hands up in the air, my parents patiently and intentionally positioned me for a meaningful and successful life.

Ultimately, I went to the same community college my mom went to, before transferring to and graduating from a four-year university. I became actively involved in organizing and politics, eventually working for President Obama's election and reelection—and had the honor of being appointed deputy director of the office of public engagement at the White House.

I made it.

But not by accident.

Of the 71 eighth graders who graduated with me from my middle school, only a handful went on to graduate from

college. With little to no formal education beyond middle school or high school, many of my classmates suffered from drug abuse and had run-ins with the law—the plight of many rural communities. My success was not in the cards.

So how did I make it? I was lucky. My parents—like all parents—wanted what was best for me and they had the fortune, over time, to give me the opportunities to realize my potential and intervene at key points to knock down obstacles or point me in the right direction. I had certain advantages, ones that all children should have—a stable caregiving environment, access to basic health care, essential meals, and a safe public school. These critical components, along with strong parent advocates, created a path for me.

Parents are their children's best advocates. Harnessing the intuitive advocacy of committed parents with the need for children's advocacy in public policy at the grassroots level is the only way we will create an environment where kids can thrive. It is this idea that has led me to run a new California-based effort launched by Common Sense Kids Action called the California Kids Campaign, aimed at building a grassroots movement of parents, teachers, and community members to make kids our state's No. 1 public policy priority.

California ranks 49 out of 50 in the nation for standard of living for kids. Roughly half of the children in the state live in families that are in or near poverty. Nearly 75 percent of our youngest kids don't receive important developmental health screenings. One in four kids don't regularly have enough food to eat. An estimated 1 million California kids don't have access to licensed child care. The barriers to opportunity and healthy child development are even greater in many communities of color. Latino and African American children are far more likely to live in poverty than white children in California.

California—the Golden State, the seventh-largest economy in the world, and a state known for its innovation and creativity—can do better. We must do better. We are failing our children, and it is time for us to stand up and demand change from our elected officials.

The goal of the California Kids Campaign is to provide the grassroots avenue of engagement for parents to become the catalysts of change for their kids. This year, we will run a parent-powered mobilization effort around ballot measures that impact kids. We will invest in a Parent Organizer program, designed to engage parents in lasting grassroots change in their communities. Building on the Kids Action Agenda that Common Sense Kids Action has been developing for the last year, we will advocate in Sacramento on issues that impact kids: high-quality early childhood, including child care, pre-K, nutrition, and preventive health care. We will support policies that address poverty and other barriers to children getting the right start and policies that support working families, such as paid sick and family and medical leave, fair pay, Earned Income and Child Tax credits, and child care benefits.

We are not partisan—we are kid-partisan. Children don't have entrenched special interest groups. There are no dark money slush funds for kids. No lobbyists on retainer. No super PACs raising millions from the ultra rich to protect society's most valuable asset—our children. But children have one very powerful wildcard—their parents. The well-being, health, and education of children will be our North Star. That is our entrenched interest.

This is a long-term effort to build an army of parent advocates. I know firsthand what is possible when parents advocate for their children's best interests—and if we can come together to collectively fight for all children in California, we can open up a world of opportunity. Please go to CAKidsCampaign.org to sign up for our campaign.

EVALUATING THE AUTHOR'S ARGUMENTS:

Viewpoint author Buffy Wicks argues that parents are the best advocates for their children. How does she support this argument? How does this compare to other articles in this chapter? Would the age and abilities of the child be a factor in determining who is the best advocate?

Viewpoint 5

Protests Are Important for Disability Activists

David M. Perry

"I feel so passionate about what we're doing that I am willing, more than willing, to get arrested for it."

In the following viewpoint, David M. Perry describes how the activist group ADAPT protested in the summer of 2017. ADAPT has been fighting for the rights of disabled people for many years. They often practice civil disobedience, a peaceful form of political protest that involves refusing to comply with certain laws or government demands. In 2017, Republican politicians attempted to cut Medicaid, a government program many disabled people depend on. The author interviews Anita Cameron, who has been participating in protests for over 30 years. She describes the process of preparing for protests. David M. Perry is a former professor of history and a freelance journalist focused on disability, parenting, education, and history.

"'That's Just the Life of a Warrior': How Disability Activists Are Playing the Long Game Under Trump," by David M. Perry, *Pacific Standard,* January 23, 2018. First published in Pacific Standard and Reprinted with permission of Pacific Standard 2018.

AS YOU READ, CONSIDER THE FOLLOWING QUESTIONS:
1. Why were disability activists protesting in 2017?
2. Why do disability activists plan and practice civil disobedience in advance, according to the interview?
3. What can activists do if they can't or don't want to protest in the streets, according to the interview?

For two or possibly three days this last summer, the entirety of American political culture was shaped by the activism of the disability rights movement. Led by the direct action group ADAPT (profiled in *Pacific Standard* first last spring and covered throughout the summer), disabled activists seized control of the narrative around Trumpcare and never really let go. As the GOP vows to return to its Trumpcare efforts in 2018, it's worth looking back at how exactly Republican attacks on Medicaid were derailed. ADAPT's presence in Washington, DC, was no accident. The group's ability to command media attention and use the power of civil disobedience came through years of practice. ADAPT has been training for this moment, but its members also recognize that this can't go on forever. Last fall, when I called up longtime ADAPTer Adam Prizio, he told me, "A system that requires heroic effort to function normally is doomed to fail."

Over the fall and winter, I've been speaking to many ADAPTers about their experiences during the "#SummerofADAPT," a hashtag and rallying cry that Prizio created in what his colleague Gregg Beratan calls a "moment of genius." The message was consistent. The actions we saw last summer were not frantic, ad-hoc efforts born of simple desperation at the assault on Medicaid—although that threat is real. Instead, ADAPTers would like to be understood as one of America's most practiced and effective civil disobedience organizations.

To tell this story and make the work behind the rallies apparent, *Pacific Standard* spoke to Anita Cameron. Among disability rights activists, Cameron is legendary. She's been performing acts of civil disobedience for almost four decades, with over 130 arrests. She also pushes the disability community to confront issues of race, class, sexuality, and other aspects of intersecting justice within its own ranks.

Disability rights advocate Anita Cameron (center) joins fellow ADAPT demonstrators to protest in Washington, DC.

Looking back on the summer, how are you feeling?

We won a couple of battles, but this war is not over. We have to remain ever vigilant, and whether they try to tuck it away in tax reform, they're going to keep trying to [cut Medicaid] until they finally give up or they get this passed. ADAPT, we're vowing to keep that from happening, so we're going to be out there fighting—and you know, if some of us have to get on the bus to go to wherever [to protest], then [we'll go].

How do you prepare for your actions?

I've been in ADAPT for over 31 years. So to me it's almost like breathing. We usually know, other than emergency actions that came up through the summer, what's coming up. We have two actions a year, usually in DC. We usually don't know exactly what we're going to be doing or where we're going to be going.

Do your protest targets know you're coming?

There has to be an element of surprise!

Usually, for me, a couple of weeks out is when the excitement starts happening. I get that excitement, and I'm preparing myself mentally for anything that may happen. And then in Rochester [New York], we get a bus and we take at least 30 folks with us. Once we get to DC, it's exciting because it's almost like a family reunion.

I'm interested in the longer-term preparation too. how do you get ready for the whole trip? What do you tell newcomers?

When the actions are coming up in the spring or the fall, about six weeks out, we have trainings every couple of weeks because we always have new people. We tell them what it's going to be like, how to pack the bags so people's stuff doesn't get thrown away. We tell them what to expect, the do's and don'ts. We tell them about civil disobedience and non-violence. Critical things like bringing your meds in a prescription bottle, in case you get arrested, [so] your meds aren't confiscated as unknown drugs.

Usually our last meeting is the week of the action, and we do a mock action. And then afterwards we go over what happened.

So you stage mock actions to practice? What are those like?

It can be anything! It's usually taking over something: An office, a bathroom, whatever, to simulate, as close as possible, what you do [in a real protest]—the adrenaline, the chaos, to give people a feel what to expect.

On Sundays [before actions] we have our legal meeting; it goes into into the history of ADAPT, civil disobedience, and why we use that. And we have published an activist guide. I wrote the part about intersectionality. I'm black. I'm disabled. I'm a lesbian. And I worked in the LGBT community before I joined ADAPT. Once I joined ADAPT, I spoke out pretty much about disability discrimination for 25 years. But when Michael Brown got killed, I really decided that, look, I can't separate my identities and my intersections of oppression from disability.

Also, we [must] pay attention to our walking folks who may be helping to open doors. The police sometimes will grab the folks who are walking. Just because you're walking doesn't mean you're non-disabled, but they'll assume the walking folks are non-disabled. They assume that if they grab the walking people, the folks in wheelchairs or mobility devices will somehow run away.

That has never happened.

No! Not in the 35 years of ADAPT has that ever happened.

We know what we're getting into. Especially us veterans who've been around a few years, a few decades. In comparison [with back then], we've got it a little easy. Back in the day, when the police really didn't have any idea of disabled folks, they'd pull us out of our wheelchairs and scream at us to walk. I used to get beat up on the regular by the police. As ADAPT grew, in many ways, and became more powerful and getting to the table more, especially in Washington, DC, the police, they weren't as likely to do that.

In this administration, police have been a little rougher with us, and our actions—just out of necessity—have been a little more grueling and intense, kind of like it was back in the day.

What don't people understand about ADAPT?

We are fierce activists who know what we're getting into. We're not some mindless lemmings following behind the pied piper. We know.

Two big things people mistake ADAPT for: That we're only for people in wheelchairs, and that you have to get arrested. We're cross-disability, and the getting arrested part is optional. We know that and we're willing to do it. I had my 132nd arrest on this action [in the fall]. I feel so passionate about what we're doing that I am willing, more than willing, to get arrested for it.

That's just the life of a warrior, a civil rights activist. These are things that one does—those of us who can get out in the trenches. We have a measure of privilege. I have a measure of privilege to be out in the streets and the trenches to get to where I need be. There are people who cannot, whether it's because of their disability, their personality issues, their job—for whatever reason, they cannot do it. Whether they are stuck at home or stuck in bed, I appreciate all forms of activism. You can't get out in the street, then sign this petition or signal-boost information. Be an observer. There's so many ways to do activism. And I think a lot of times in the disability community in general, we sometimes forget that, or it's a measure of ableism on our part; but not everybody can get out in the street.

What's coming next?

We are trying to get co-sponsors for the Disability Integration Act. The act is legislation that will give people with disabilities the right to live in the community with the services and supports that they need. Our previous bills (Community First Choice, etc.) were written for Medicaid programs. This was written in a civil rights framework: It's the civil right of people with disabilities to live in the community. The bill addresses transportation, housing, services, and supports in the community. Insurance companies will have to pay. It's a bipartisan bill with bipartisan support. ADAPT is non-partisan. We pick on Democrats and Republicans and independents all equally.

If you're messing with our civil rights, you're going to hear from ADAPT.

EVALUATING THE AUTHOR'S ARGUMENTS:

In this viewpoint, David M. Perry interviews an activist who promotes civil disobedience. Is this a form of self-advocacy? What are the advantages and disadvantages to public protests when it comes to supporting the rights of disabled people?

Chapter 3

How Can You Be a Good Advocate?

There are a number of skills and characteristics that make for an effective advocate.

Successful Advocacy Requires Preparation

"Effective advocacy does more than whine. Good advocacy helps to define the outcome you want to achieve."

Mark Sweet

In the following excerpted viewpoint, Mark Sweet offers advice for successful advocating. He discusses the importance of first thinking about your current life and then considering changes you might want. He lists strategies for preparing for and conducting discussions. He notes that personalities and emotions can get in the way of successful discussions. Being prepared for these challenges can help people overcome them. The most important factor is to always keep in mind the needs and wishes of the person with the disability. Mark Sweet is a trainer and consultant with Disability Rights Wisconsin.

AS YOU READ, CONSIDER THE FOLLOWING QUESTIONS:

1. Why is it important to know what you want before you decide on an advocacy plan?
2. What is the difference between an outcome and a method?
3. What can happen when people get upset during discussions?

"Becoming an Effective Advocate," by Mark Sweet, Disability Rights Wisconsin. Reprinted by permission.

Advocating for oneself requires a great deal of research, but help is available.

To advocate means to take action, to do something in order to make something else happen. There are different kinds of advocacy. "Systems advocacy" is to influence the way things are done for everyone in a county, a school district, or a state. "Individual advocacy" is to influence what happens for one person, which could be yourself. This chapter is primarily about individual advocacy.

Some people talk about advocacy as speaking up or standing up for yourself or someone else. Advocacy is better understood as action taken to effect a desired change or outcome. Effective advocacy does more than whine. Good advocacy helps to define the outcome you want to achieve. In this section, we will explore some aspects of tying action to a desired outcome.

Some advocacy is about "rights." The law requires that eligible people have certain opportunities and services available to them in a timely manner. When those opportunities, services, or time lines are not honored, this represents a violation of legal or procedural rights.

FAST FACT

People should learn to advocate for themselves as early as possible. Learning and practicing self advocacy when young sets people up for successful lives.

There are other aspects of service, support, or accommodation that are not legal requirements but would help to make a person's life better. These things could also be the focus of a person's advocacy efforts.

Advocating for Yourself

What do you want? Some people know the answer to that question. Others, when asked, "What do you want?" or "What is your dream?" do not know the answer, at least not right away. Advocating for what you want is a process that starts with considering your life as it is. Where do you live and who lives with you? Where do you work and what do you do there? Who are the friends and other people in your life? What do you do for fun, or want to do? Where do you go, or would you like to go? What personal, material, and technical accommodations might be helpful in your life?

Consider your life. Some people find it helpful to talk about their lives while others might find it easier to avoid language initially. If you like, try drawing whatever comes to mind related to each topic (i.e., home, work, people, fun, places, and accommodations) on a piece of paper. The purpose is not to include every detail or to create great art. Rather, it is to help you consider your life as it is. Whatever comes to mind, say it, and write it down (or ask someone you trust to write it down). Or, draw first and then describe what you have drawn.

What else do I want? What else might help? After you describe your life as it is, think about what else you might want or what you would like to change. Try to fill in a blank, for example, "When I consider work, I want ___." Or, "When I consider the people in my life, I want ___." This kind of consideration can lead to some desired outcomes, some wants. Because advocacy means taking action, once you know what outcome you want, then you can make a plan.

Invite an ally. You can ask someone to work with you. Hopefully, no one has to pursue advocacy goals alone. An ally is someone you trust. An ally can be another advocate, a friend or coworker, or a family member. An ally is someone who will listen to what you want, rather than tell you what you need. An ally can ask good questions that help you to be clear about your goals.

Make a plan. Think about your desired outcome and ask, "What can I do to get started?" Is there someone to tell? Is there a request to make known? Is there information to get? Are there skills to learn? Think of many things that you could do, and then decide what you will do first. If you get stuck, ask someone you trust to help you figure out what to try first. And then do it.

Advocating for Someone Else

Make every effort to include the person in the process. Some people will be able to actively communicate with you about their advocacy goals using language. Others will communicate what they enjoy and do not enjoy by their actions; what they want more or less of. When someone does not have ease of communication, pay attention to the person's affect. Under what conditions do you witness the most positive participation as compared to dullness or distress. Advocate for outcomes the person values.

When advocating for someone else, it is very important to keep the person at the center of your efforts. It is sometimes a challenge to keep personalities off to the side. Try not to get lost in personal struggles. You do not have to agree with other opinions or like the way everyone else communicates. Do not let your personal dislike for someone interfere with your efforts on behalf of the person who wants a change through advocacy.

General Advocacy Strategies

Distinguish outcomes from methods. There is a difference between an outcome and a method of achieving it. Improved communication between a person with a disability and others is an outcome. Improved communication at work and in a restaurant, are focused outcomes. Speech therapy is a method. Use of picture cards or a computer to communicate are methods. Clarify your outcomes before you invest too much time and energy on one specific method. Attention to communication throughout a person's day (or specifically at work and in the restaurant) can be more effective for some people than time with a therapist a few times a week. You might invest a lot of time advocating for a method, get it, and still not achieve the desired outcome. First, decide on the desired outcome. Then, consider methods that might be the best match for the person. In other words, avoid wasting valuable time debating one set of street directions versus another, when you are not certain about the destination.

There are several ways to prepare yourself. Be aware of your personal sensitivities. Notice the kinds of comments or actions by others that you can predict will upset or anger you. Ask yourself what you hope will not happen in a meeting (because it probably will). Many advocates say they lose focus and effectiveness when certain things happen because they become too upset. In order not to be surprised and thrown off balance, make note of the things you hope will not happen, that are likely to upset you, and then just check them off when they happen. Exhale. Take a short break. Take care of yourself.

Know the players. Learn who is involved in making decisions, what each person's role and responsibilities are. Know who has the authority to make decisions and make contact with the right person. If there is an order of authority, respect it. However, if you are not satisfied at one level, inform that person that while you appreciate their time or help so far, you will be contacting another person as well. While there will be people along the advocacy path who you might not enjoy or who do not offer the help you want, it is also true that people will not leave their jobs because you do not like them or their decisions. Parents, educators and administrators, county workers, and others all might be around for a long time. This should not dissuade you from advocating, but remind you that you can respectfully disagree.

Use questions to invite discussion. People who disagree tend to argue or be silenced by someone else's position. Avoid becoming polarized. One of the best ways to avoid becoming locked into opposing positions is to ask questions. When you feel ready to pounce or withdraw, ask a question instead. Asking questions does not mean that you are conceding; it means that you are willing to understand another perspective. Be curious. The better you understand what someone else is and is not considering the more able you will be to work with the information.

Focus. Advocacy is about someone's life. Keep the focus of discussion on the relevant person. Ask any speaker to directly connect suggestions to what is known about a specific person, and do the same yourself. Something that might be a good idea for one person, might not be a good idea for another. Discuss how a proposal does or does not match what is known about this one person.

Individualize. Represent the person you are advocating for in terms of learning and performances characteristics, temperament, what the person values, communication methods and style, what brings on a smile, etc. Avoid the short cut of using diagnostic labels or measures of severity (e.g., mild, moderate, profound) to make support or program decisions. When participation, rather than total independence, is a valued outcome, most things are possible for an individual.

Seek outcomes that enhance a person's participation in all aspects of life. Think in terms of functional options. A functional option means that if the person does not achieve more than this one outcome, s/he will still be participating in ordinary daily life. Avoid goals that remove or hold someone back from ordinary daily life and places until "prerequisite skills" have been mastered. Special places and activities that are supposed to lead to more functional participation in life are not as solid a foundation as regular places and regular activities that could be emphasized immediately with the proper support for participation. Participation in ordinary activities is the best foundation for continued and improved participation in ordinary activities.

Document. Keep a written record of your requests and the decisions that are made before leaving meetings. Document your understanding of what will be done next, who will be responsible, and how much time will be taken. Follow verbal exchanges in person or on the phone with memos reflecting your understanding of things.

Actively participate. Most advocacy is ongoing. If you want a particular topic brought up, or time to speak at a meeting, contact the person who leads the meetings you attend so that these requests can be made part of the agenda. Ask for and provide explanations and examples when you want to achieve more clarity. A simple request, such as "please say that in another way" or "please provide an example of what you mean" could make a positive difference for you. If you are nervous about interrupting, try it anyway. It will get easier.

Be selective about the issues you challenge. What is the advocacy issue you want to pursue? When there is disagreement about methods, remember that there is always more than one way to achieve a desired outcome. Consider trying something other than your first choice (or asking someone else to try something) for a set period of time, and then notice the value of that method. Unless it is harmful to do so, be flexible.

Avoid asking "why?" People in advocacy disputes often say they dislike when others become defensive. Asking someone why something was done is an invitation to defend a position. Questions that begin with the word "why" invite defensiveness. If you want to understand, ask "how" a decision was made. What were the considerations?

[...]

EVALUATING THE AUTHOR'S ARGUMENTS:

In this viewpoint, Mark Sweet focuses on methods of successful advocacy. Preparing well and staying calm are key. How could these techniques improve results? What might happen if people don't follow this author's recommendations?

Choosing the Right Advocate Takes Time and Effort

Kim Davis

> *"Just as finding the right doctor, teacher, or therapist takes time and investigation, so too should obtaining an advocate."*

In the following viewpoint, Kim Davis argues that it is important to properly investigate when choosing an advocate. She notes the ways a family can benefit from having a good professional advocate. Yet because the advocate is such an important part of the team, an inexperienced advocate or a poor fit can do more harm than good. She suggests questions to ask in order to determine if the advocate is going to be helpful. These questions and guidelines are designed to help a family choose an appropriate advocate for a child with special needs. Kim Davis works with the Indiana Institute on Disability and Community.

AS YOU READ, CONSIDER THE FOLLOWING QUESTIONS:
1. What are advantages to working with a professional advocate?
2. Why is it important for someone needing an advocate to choose carefully?
3. Why is objectivity an important quality for a professional advocate?

Choosing an advocate is an important undertaking, whether on behalf of yourself or others, such as children or family members, and should not be done quickly or carelessly.

How does this pertain to families who have a son or daughter with a disability? Many times the systems in which families find themselves (e.g., early intervention, school, adult agency) can be overwhelming and confusing. Add increased emotions to the mix, and it is often hard for family members to think clearly and rationally in the heat of a meeting in which they are asked to make crucial life decisions. To make those meetings and situations more manageable and less overwhelming, an advocate may be "employed" to assist, encourage, or educate a family in understanding the ramifications of their decisions. The right advocate at the right moment can have a lasting impact on everyone involved, including the family, the staff of professionals supporting the individual with disabilities, and ultimately, the individual with the disability. That impact can be positive or negative. An advocate is not a person to simply choose without thought and discussion. The wrong advocate can have a serious impact on the relationship between the family and agency. That relationship may likely be longer lasting than the relationship the family may have with the advocate!! Just as finding the right doctor, teacher, or therapist takes time and investigation, so too should obtaining an advocate.

What Is an Advocate and What Do They Do?

According to the dictionary, advocate means "to speak in favor of, one who supports a cause, or one who speaks in another's behalf" (Webster's New College Dictionary, 1999). There are several roles or functions that an advocate may play in supporting a child with a disability and his or her family. They may include:

- Listening to all parties in a believing and nonjudgmental manner;
- Clarifying issues;
- Suggesting options;
- Documenting;
- Locating and providing information;
- Modeling appropriate behaviors and boundaries;
- Speaking on the parent/child's behalf when they cannot speak for themselves;
- Helping the family with written correspondence or phone calls;
- Attending meetings;
- Problem solving;
- Educating families;
- Assisting parents in locating other supports; and
- Following up.

The advocate is NOT a therapist, a lawyer, or the primary decision maker (IN-Source correspondence, December 2005).

Why Would One Obtain an Advocate?

As suggested by the list of functions an advocate may play, a family might consider working with an advocate when they feel overwhelmed with the amount and type of information they are receiving, if they need assistance in correspondence or locating additional supports, and/or if they need help with problem solving when issues are challenging and it becomes hard to maintain emotions while attending meetings. Clearly, an advocate can become an invaluable asset to a family and a child with a disability. At the same time, an advocate can also become a detriment or disadvantage unless the family is careful and thoughtful in choosing their advocate and maintaining their services.

Choosing an Advocate

Since an advocate has the ability to become an integral part of a child's educational team, it is vital for the family to do research prior to obtaining an advocate. Simply because someone calls him or herself an advocate, does not mean he or she always represents the family and child in the best possible manner. Research can assist in finding the right person who ultimately can help or hinder the future of your child. Consider the following information seeking guidelines:

What Type of Training in Special Education and School Systems Has This Person Received?

Training is available to advocates. It would be useful to find out what training the potential advocate has received. What topics were covered that would make someone an advocate? What skills were stressed? Skills such as communication, collaboration, presentation, and maintaining a professional relationship are important skills needed by anyone who is an advocate. When and where were the trainings and how long were they? How frequently does the advocate attend trainings? They should have current information and a good knowledge of special education in general as well as special education law. Care must be taken to ensure that their information is current and accurate. Practical experience such as attending IEP meetings or case conference participation should also be expected. Remember, knowledge alone does not make an effective and good advocate, interpersonal skills are essential in order to create and maintain a good working, collaborative relationship.

How Long Has This Person Been Involved in Advocacy?

When did he or she become an advocate? If the person has been involved for a long time they may have established relationships with certain school districts; this can be good or bad depending upon the advocates approach. There are advantages to being an advocate for a long time such as getting to know the systems as well as people within the systems. However, reputations can be positive or negative. Someone who is new to being an advocate will not have a reputation that can either tarnish or enhance their usefulness, but he or she can bring along the current training and knowledge that is needed.

Does This Person Understand YOUR Child and Your Child's Needs?

It is important for any advocate to get to know YOUR child and YOUR child's needs and not compare your child to another. Even children who have the same or similar diagnosis deserve to be treated as individuals. It may be wise to have the advocate meet your child and spend some time together before any conferences. In that way, the advocate can better assist you in tailoring your requests to the unique needs of your child. There are no recipes or simple methods that can be used with every child. Each situation is different and requires open minds to come up with solutions for the distinguishing features of your child. The advocate should be able to explain how your child's disability may impact their learning and then work with you to help prioritize your child's needs. Each child is an individual and therefore, deserves to be considered as an individual and not as a part of a group who share a label.

Will This Person Be Sensitive to the Fact That YOU Have the Ultimate Final Decision Making Power?

An advocate can offer options for different situations but must respect you to make the final decision. An advocate who interjects too much personal preference is overstepping his or her role. Ultimately, decisions are for the parents to make when given options. An advocate knows and expects this. The parent makes the final decision, not the advocate.

Can This Person Be Objective? What Evidence Is There of This Fact?

Having an open mind is an asset for everyone participating in meetings that discuss the future of a child. There are many options. An advocate should not be influenced by personal experiences or relationships with a school system that would impact his or her emotions and reason. This is not about them and their history, but it is about YOUR child.

If there is a history and the advocate cannot be objective, it may not be a good match for you and your child.

Can This Person Maintain a Professional Demeanor?

Professional demeanor may be hard to define in exact terms, but most of us would think of words such as respectful, courteous, competent, open-minded, or considerate as part of the definition. An advocate should embody all of those traits when supporting you and your child. Once again, it would be imperative for the advocate to separate "personal" from "professional" issues when working with you, in order to keep your child's best interest foremost and not their personal agenda. If an advocate performs in an un-professional manner, it can do more harm than good for your relationship with the school and, ultimately, for your child.

Does This Person Seek Win-Win Solutions?

When an advocate is utilized, there is usually a perceived need on the part of the family for additional support in understanding systems or working with the school to create an acceptable program. Can your advocate work collaboratively to achieve a win—win solution that supports your child, but does not put the school in a financial or personnel strain? While you may want "everything" for your child, every other parent who has a child in special education does too. It is impossible for any school district to give "everything" to every child.

Does the advocate recognize the limits of the system, as well as the limits of the family, or ask questions that would lead to a mutual satisfactory solution? Does the advocate work to avoid the "us/them" situation which only creates tension and ill will? That is a more collaborative and reasonable way to achieve a desired goal. Suggesting the tabling of a toxic issue until more information can be generated and gathered may prove to be more helpful than pushing forward when an issue becomes questionable. Ultimately over time, working collaboratively will garner more for your child and your family.

Does This Person Understand His/Her Professional Limits?

An advocate is not an attorney. An advocate should know when to stop, because their role has started to switch from being a support person to someone giving legal advice. Then it is time to suggest an attorney. Most advocates should have an attorney who they are familiar with and who they can recommend to families.

What References Are Available and What Is the Reputation of This Advocate?

Just as families would seek references and reputation information for medical or other personnel, seeking information about an advocate is wise. Simply because someone calls him or herself an advocate does not mean they are qualified.

You may want to seek information from other families and the school districts where the advocate has been working. Questions to ask may be: How many meetings has the advocate attended and how did they work in those meetings; collaboratively or as an adversary? Do schools see the advocate as someone who complains, always finds an issue because the schools are out to "get" students with disabilities, generates undue stress, and threatens lawsuits? Do families feel comfortable with the demeanor and manner in which the advocate "represents" them to the school? Do families and schools see the advocate as someone who is open-minded and willing to negotiate or someone who has an agenda in each instance? Careful consideration of the choice of an advocate can make or break the relationship between the school and your family.

Can This Person Help You Build and Maintain a Good, Trusting, Positive Relationship for YOU with Your Child's School?

Your child will be in his or her school daily for many years to come. Teachers and staff talk to one another and share their insights and feelings, just as families do. Teachers want to do what is best for all of the students they serve. But, a strained relationship can "drain" their physical and emotional resources and thus impact the type of care and services a student receives. A fear-based relationship may not be the best way to achieve the goals set forth for a child! This happens not because teachers/staff are bad people, but because they are human and the added stress and tension can adversely affect their work with a child. It is not intentional, but it can happen.

As in life, an advocate should help you achieve a positive relationship with your child's school. The saying, "you can get more with sugar than you can with vinegar" holds true in so many ways. If you work with the school, realize their limits and try to collaborate with them for the good of your child, you will achieve more in the long run than if you make unreasonable demands simply because an advocate says to do it. When we have positive and healthy relationships in our lives, we are more apt to get things accomplished and done for us because others genuinely care about our welfare and that of our child and family.

We need to have positive, strong, and nurturing relationships all of our lives to assist us in meeting our needs and those of our children. Without strong and positive relationships, achieving our goals may be challenging. The future of your child is in your ability to choose your battles wisely, understand constraints, and seek ways to "add a little sugar" to the relationships you create. Let's make this relationship work to your child's advantage.

EVALUATING THE AUTHOR'S ARGUMENTS:

Viewpoint author Kim Davis discusses the possible benefits and pitfalls of working with a professional advocate. Given this information, would you conclude that a professional advocate is an important part of the team for someone with special needs? Why or why not?

Understanding Your Rights Is Essential

> *"It is important to remember that not all behavior we don't like is against the law or a formal policy that can be enforced."*

Disability Rights Wisconsin

In the following excerpted viewpoint, authors from Disability Rights Wisconsin note that some rights are protected by law and others are not. Even if a right is not covered by the law, it may be covered by contracts or policies. People may also claim they have rights based on society's expectations. The authors provide an exercise to help people determine what may be a right versus a preference. Knowing the difference is important to determine how to demand a right. It may be difficult to navigate the complex system, but educating yourself is an essential step. Disability Rights Wisconsin provides free advocacy services to Wisconsin residents with disabilities.

AS YOU READ, CONSIDER THE FOLLOWING QUESTIONS:
1. What defines a legal right?
2. How can a contract or policy provide certain rights?
3. What are social rights and what can we do to enforce them?

"Advocacy Tool Kit Skills and Strategies for Effective Self and Peer Advocacy," Disability Rights Wisconsin. Reprinted by permission.

Some rights are guaranteed under the law and others are simply societal expectations. Understanding the law and other policies will help you fight for your rights.

I n the United States, we all have rights as citizens. As people with disabilities, we have often been led to believe that we don't have rights or should be afraid to exercise them. Some rights are governed by laws or rules, while others are not. Therefore the term "rights" can sometimes be confusing. It is important to understand the differences in the types of rights that you may have so that you can determine the best advocacy strategy. To do this, let's first identify different types of rights.

Laws: Some rights that we have are legal rights, and therefore may be enforceable in a court of law or through a formal grievance procedure. There can be Federal, State, or local laws. For example, a federal law called the Health Insurance Portability and Accountability Act of 1996 (HIPAA) makes it illegal in most instances for a health care provider to share your private health care information with others.

Therefore, according to this law, you have the right to private health care records.

Contracts: You can also have rights under a contract that are enforceable through a court of law. One example of a contract is a rental lease. A lease outlines the rights and responsibilities of tenants. If you feel your rights under a lease have been violated, your case can be heard in small claims court.

Rules and Policies: Sometimes there are rules or policies that outline your rights. The rules or policies may not be law, but may be governed by law or may simply be a set of guidelines that an agency or an individual claims to follow. In either case, if a rule or policy has been broken, there typically is a way to file a complaint or formal grievance to address your concern. For example, your doctor may have a policy that states that you have up to 30 days to pay the balance of your bill.

Preferences and Social Expectations: Every society has a set of social expectations or rules that are followed, and everyone has personal preferences in how they would like to be treated. Preferences and social expectations are typically not illegal, and therefore are not the same as a right that someone has under a law or a policy. It is very important to understand the differences between enforceable rights—rights that are governed by a policy or law—and things that we may refer to as being a "right," but that are not covered under any law or policy. For example, how often have you said or heard people say "I have the right to be listened to" or "I have the right to make a mistake." Although expressed as rights, the right to be listened to or the right to make a mistake are really preferences of how we would like to be treated, and they are not likely to be a right we have under a policy or law.

It is important to remember that not all behavior we don't like is against the law or a formal policy that can be enforced. This does not mean that you cannot address a concern you have about being treated rudely. For example, let's say you were stood up two times by someone who is coming to give you an estimate on painting your bedroom. Although they did not break any law by making you wait for them, you could call or write a letter to the owner of the business letting then know that you were dissatisfied with how you were treated. Writing a letter or placing a phone call may or may not change the painter's behavior.

Exercise:

Can you pick out what might be considered a law versus a social expectation or preference versus a rule or policy versus a contract? There may be more than one answer to the question. Take a few minutes to complete this exercise:

1. The right to employment without discrimination based on disability, under the Wisconsin Fair Employment Act.

2. The right to be happy.

3. The right to be "treated with dignity and respect" by your physical therapist as identified by the rehabilitation facility where she works.

4. The right to have a painter complete painting your house, as identified in the agreement.

5. The right to not be abused by your home health care aide.

6. The right to say "I don't know."

7. The right to seek housing without discrimination based on disability, under the Fair Housing Amendments Act.

8. The right to choose your health care provider.*

* **Answers:**

1. The Wisconsin Fair Employment Act is a law.

2. The right to be happy is generally considered a preference.

3. The right to be treated with dignity and respect in a rehabilitation facility might be governed under a rule or policy set by the rehabilitation facility, and being treated with dignity and respect is also a social expectation.

4. The right to have a painter complete a job she or he promised in an agreement is governed by a contract.

5. The right not to be abused by your home health care aide is a right that is governed by a rule and policy and is against the law!

6. The right to say "I don't know" is considered a preference.

7. The Fair Housing Amendments Act is a law.

8. The right to choose your health care provider may be governed by a rule or policy, however, not necessarily. To some it may be considered a preference.

When you still have questions or need more information, how can you go gather additional facts. Finding an answer to your question is as simple as contacting the right person. You'll be surprised with the amount of progress you can make by placing a few phone calls. Even if the first person you call cannot answer your question, they are likely to point you in the right direction. Some useful places to start include: the protection and advocacy (P&A) organization for Wisconsin (Disability Rights Wisconsin); the Wisconsin Department of Health and Family Services; consumer groups; drop-in centers; and Social Security offices.

The Internet is another tool. You can search the Internet on various topics of interest, or use it to find phone numbers to local, state, or national resources. If you don't have access to the Internet at home, try a local library, many of which now offer Internet access. If you need help learning how to use the Internet, you can ask a librarian for help. Additionally, many disability- run organizations now offer both

Internet access and training. If you are more familiar with how to use the Internet, you can also see if there is a coffee shop nearby that has Internet access. Many coffee shops offer free access.

The next question is who are the key decision-makers in your situation? Often, going straight to a decision-maker can result in a decision without hassle. If you are not sure who has the authority to make the decision, ask!

Advocating for yourself takes effort. Surrounding yourself with people who can help you can make all the difference. Ask from friends, family, other advocates, professionals and others to support your efforts to navigate the system and can listen and give advice when you are frustrated.

EVALUATING THE AUTHORS' ARGUMENTS:

In this viewpoint Disability Rights Wisconsin maintains that a phone call can often answer questions and solve problems. Compare this to viewpoint 1 in this chapter. That author recommended more extensive preparation for advocacy. When might each method best be used?

Viewpoint

4

Students Must Be Self Advocates to Succeed in Higher Education

Tadesse Abera Tedla

> *"Too often, students with disabilities are supported using a dependency model and don't develop the skills to advocate for their own learning needs."*

In the following excerpted viewpoint, Tadesse Abera Tedla discusses the challenges students with disabilities face in their education after high school. As these students go to higher education institutions, they may not have their parents' help with advocacy. Colleges and universities may offer support services such as counseling centers, but students need to know when and how to make use of these options. In this academic paper, the author explores research done to date. This leads her to conclude that students who are able to advocate for themselves have more success. Tadesse Abera Tedla. is in the Department of Special Needs and Inclusive Education at the University of Gondar in Ethiopia.

AS YOU READ, CONSIDER THE FOLLOWING QUESTIONS:
1. What challenges "from within" do students with disabilities face, according to the author?
2. When should young people be taught to become self-advocates, according to the article?
3. What personal qualities help a student achieve success in higher education, according to the author?

The transition from high schools to higher education institutions can be especially difficult for students with disabilities as the impetus for securing necessary accommodations falls on students themselves rather than on parents or on the institution as it did in high schools. Students with disabilities are still facing issues in both their transition to higher education institutions and their retention to complete a degree or certificate. Educators and researchers suggest that self-advocacy skills would address the issue. A self-advocacy skill is an evidence-based predictor in secondary transition, having an impact on improved post-school outcomes in education and employment.

[…]

The Lack of Self-Advocacy Skills and Its Consequences

As an increasing number of students with disabilities enroll in Higher Education Institutions, discovering ways to best meet these students' needs becomes more pressing. The transition from high schools to higher education institutions can be especially difficult for students with disabilities as the impetus for securing necessary accommodations falls on students themselves rather than on parents or on the institution as it did in high schools. Many higher education institutions have responded to students' needs by implementing program to teach self-advocacy skills. But, few of these programs have established assessment plans to evaluate their effectiveness.[1,2,3,4] Unfortunately, all too often students with disabilities enter higher education institutions lacking understanding of how their disability affects their learning.[5,6,7,8] As a result, these students are not able to effectively articulate

Even though fighting for accessibility or other rights may be daunting, you can find help and support to get what you need to obtain a quality education.

the services and supports needed to meet the academic challenges in higher education institutions. Furthermore, students may never learn how to advocate for themselves when advocacy is done for them by others.[9] In addition to this, as[10] reported that teachers also indicated that, while more pressure was placed on academic achievement and assessments, there was less time to develop functional skills such as self-advocacy skills to students with disabilities that can help them advocate for their rights to receive better access to services and supports in schooling institutions. Hence, students with disabilities are still facing issues in both their transition to higher education institutions and their retention to complete a degree or certificate.[1] Supporting this idea,[11] affirmed that for students with disabilities in higher institutions, communicating rights and requesting appropriate accommodations have been found as areas of weakness. And, therefore, researchers concluded that students with disabilities should be urged to recognize and advocate for their needs and wants in higher education institutions.[12] It is the fact that, students with disabilities face challenges from within (e.g. low self esteem, low self-efficacy, anxiety and stress and the like), as well as from the higher education institution settings they join (e.g. lack of facilities, resources and inaccessible environment). Students with disabilities oftentimes perceive themselves as unprepared for the increased rigor of higher education. This can lead to anxiety and difficulties with academic expectations which can all lead to decreased retention rates[13,14] and they suggested that self-advocacy skills would address the issue. Again they stated that self-advocacy includes having a concept of purpose, thorough goal setting, plan development, being able to articulate personal learning needs, and persistence despite challenges. These concepts are crucial for students with disabilities if they are to succeed in higher education institutions.[15] Self-advocacy skills need to be explicitly taught to students, preferably at a young age. Too often, students with disabilities are supported using a dependency model in elementary and high school and don't develop the skills to advocate for their own learning needs.[5]

Educators Recommendation on Augmenting Self-Advocacy Skills of Students with Disabilities in Higher Education

Indeed, therefore, educators for example[1] stated that, special education researchers continue to examine the self-advocacy skills of students with disabilities that can advance our understanding of how best to meet the self-advocacy skills needs of students as they transition to higher education institutions that can serve as predictors of improved outcomes for higher education students with disabilities. Supporting this idea[16] clearly stated that among other factors, the attitude and self-advocacy skills of students with disabilities may be two of the most important factors in determining their success or failure in higher education or work related environment. They further suggested that, students with disabilities need to be prepared to work collaboratively with all interested parties and coordinators, to enable them to have an equal opportunity to participate in an institution's programs and activities. In line with this, it is better to see those empirical evidences that show how much self-advocacy skills are important to students with disabilities in higher education institutions to better maximize their education as put in below.

The Importance of Self-Advocacy Skills for a Full Inclusion in Higher Education[17]

Correlational research in the field of special education has identified self-advocacy skills as an evidence-based predictor in secondary transition, having an impact on improved post-school outcomes in education and employment.[18] In USA in their study to evaluate the efficacy of using a computer-mediated instructional strategy (the Self-Advocacy skills) to teach secondary students, identified as having an intellectual disability found out that the students learned a self-advocacy strategy and were able to demonstrate use of the strategy across settings. Furthermore,[19] and [20] in their research has found out that students with better self-advocacy skills to shape their own chosen outcomes have an easy employment after graduation. In addition to this,[21] they concluded in their study those students who were aware of and used self advocacy skills reported higher secondary graduation

rates and higher education graduation rates.[22] in his study came
out with an elaborated explanation to the case at hand. He
clearly pointed out those factors
known to support the likeli-
hood of graduating from higher
education institutions for students with disabilities. These are;
Active use of support services on
campus (e.g. writing center, counseling center, student advisement,
etc.); Forming strong relationships/mentorships with either a professional in the students office for disabilities or a faculty member
on campus; Having family support throughout the entire academic
experience; Being academically and socially involved on campus,
especially in the case of social integration; Personal qualities within
the student including self-awareness, perseverance, focus, and interpersonal skills; and Being able to self-advocate to obtain accommodations or other needs on campus.

[...]

Conclusion/Implication

Finally, though making higher institutions to be inclusive for students
with disabilities is the responsibility of higher education communities
and other stakeholders, students with disabilities are also expected to
play a role (by using self-advocacy skills) to get appropriate services
and supports to complete their education with better academic and
psycho-social achievement that enable them to be competitive in the
world of job and social integration. Supporting this idea, for example,[32] clearly stated that in higher education institution settings, it is
the responsibility of all students to advocate for themselves and their
won specific needs. However, oftentimes students with disabilities
have difficulties in this regards or they may try to have the skills after
the students have already come up against many potential obstacles
such as difficulty interacting with peers, instructors and administrators who may not be aware of the students' needs.[32]

> **FAST FACT**
>
> The Americans with Disabilities Act states that postsecondary institutions must provide necessary accommodations when a student discloses a disability.

Notes

1. Hilary, L.K. (2006) Self-Advocacy Program Self-Advocacy Programs for College Students with Disabilities: A Framework for Assessment. Annual Meeting of the American Educational Research Association, San Francisco, 7-11 April 2006.

2. Janiga, S.J., and Costenbader, V. (2002) The Transition from High School to Postsecondary Education for Students with Learning Disabilities: A Survey of College Service Coordinators. Journal of Learning Disabilities, 35, 462-468, 479. https://doi.org/10.1177/00222194020350050601.

3. Skinner, M.E., and Lindstrom, B.D. (2003) Bridging the Gap between High School and College: Strategies for the Successful Transition of Students with Learning Disabilities. Preventing School Failure, 47, 132-137. https://doi.org/10.1080/10459880309604441.

4. Smith, S.G., English, R., and Vasek, D. (2002) Student and Parent Involvement in the Transition Process for College Freshmen with Learning Disabilities. College Student Journal, 36, 491-503.

5. Brinkerhoff, L.C., McGuire, J.M., and Shaw, S.F. (2002) Postsecondary Education and Transition for Students with Learning Disabilities. 2nd Edition, Pro-Ed., Austin.

6. Getzel, E.E., and Briel, L.W. (2006) Pursuing Postsecondary Education Opportunities for Individuals with Disabilities. In: Wehman, P., Ed., Life beyond the Classroom: Transition Strategies for Young People with Disabilities, Paul H. Brookes, Baltimore, 355-368.

7. Getzel, E.E., and McManus, S. (2005) Expanding Support Services on Campus. In: Getzel, E.E., and Wehman, P., Eds., Going to College: Expanding Opportunities for People with Disabilities, Paul H. Brookes. Baltimore, 139-154.

8. Wagner, M., Newman, L., Cameto, R., Garza, N., and Levine, P. (2005) After High School: A First Look at the Postschool Experiences of Youth with Disabilities. A Report from the National Longitudinal Transition Study-2 (NLTS2).

9. Brinckerhoff, L.C. (1993) Self-Advocacy: A Critical Skill for College Students with Learning Disabilities. Family and Community Health, 16, 23-33. https://doi.org/10.1097/00003727-199310000-00005.

10. Schelling, A. (2010) Evaluating the Use of a Self-Advocacy Strategy as a Means of Improving Progress in the General Curriculum for Individuals with Cognitive Disabilities. Ed.D. Dissertation, Western Michigan University, Michigan.

11. Swanson, C. (2008) Special Education in America: The State of Students with Disabilities in the Nation's High Schools. Editorial Projects in Education Research Center, Bethesda. http://www.edweek.org/media/eperc_specialeducationinamerica.pdf.

12. Wagner, M., Marder, C., Blackorby, J., Cameto, R., Newman, L., Levine, P., and Davies-Mercier, E. (2003) The Achievements of Youth with Disabilities during Secondary School: A Report from the National Longitudinal Transition Study-2 (NLTS2). SRI International, Menlo Park. www.nlts2.org/reports/2003_11/nlts2_report_2003_11_execsum.pdf.

13. Reed, M.J., Kennett, D.J., Lewis, T., Lund-Lucas, E., Stallberg, C., and Newbold, I.L. (2009) The Relative Effects of University Success Courses and Individualized Interventions for Students with Learning Disabilities. Higher Education Research and Development, 28, 385-400. https://doi.org/10.1080/07294360903067013.

14. Connor, D.J. (2012) Helping Students with Disabilities Transition to College. Teaching Exceptional Children, 44, 16-25. https://doi.org/10.1177/004005991204400502.

15. Mamiseishvili, K., and Koch, L.C. (2011) First-to-Second-Year Persistence of Students with Disabilities in Postsecondary Institutions in the United States. Rehabilitation Counseling Bulletin, 54, 93-105. https://doi.org/10.1177/0034355210382580.

16. Mpofu, E., Hawkins, T., Bishop, M., Charema, J., Moswela, E., and Ntinda, K. (2010) Career Counseling of People with Disability. In: Kobus, M., Ed., Career Counseling: Methods That Work, Juta, Cape Town, 34-44.

17. Test, D.W., Fowler, C., and Kohler, P. (2013) Evidence-Based Practices and Predictors in Secondary Transition: What We Know and What We Still Need to Know. National Secondary Transition Technical Assistance Center, Charlotte.

18. Schelling, A.L., and Rao, S. (2013) Evaluating Self-Advocacy Strategy Instruction for Students with an Intellectual Disability Using an Interactive Hypermedia Program. International Journal of Business and Social Science, 4, 1-10.

19. Hadre, P.L., and Reeve, J. (2003) A Motivational Model of Rural Students' Intentions to Persist in, versus Drop out of, High School. Journal of Educational Psychology, 95, 347-356. https://doi.org/10.1037/0022-0663.95.2.347.

20. Zhang, D., and Law, B.H. (2005) Self-Determination as a Dropout Prevention Strategy. Journal of at Risk Issues, 11, 25-31.

21. Anctil, T., Ishikawa, M., and Scott, A. (2008) Academic Identity Development through Self-Determination: Successful College Students with Learning Disabilities. Career Development for Exceptional Individuals, 31, 164-174. https://doi.org/10.1177/0885728808315331.

22. Barber, P. (2012) College Students with Disabilities: What Factors Influence Successful Degree Completion? A Case Study. Disability and Work Research Report.

32. Lynch, R.T., and Gussel, L. (1996) Disclosure and Self-Advocacy Regarding Disability-Related Needs: Strategies to Maximize Integration in Post Secondary Education. Journal of Counseling and Development, 74, 352-357. https://doi.org/10.1002/j.1556-6676.1996.tb01879.

EVALUATING THE AUTHOR'S ARGUMENTS:

Viewpoint author Tadesse Abera Tedla argues that young people with special needs must be their own advocates. How does this compare to the viewpoints that recommend parents or professional advocates? Considering all these options, what would you conclude is the best means of advocacy?

Viewpoint 5

I Succeeded by Being My Own Advocate

Joseph D. Robbins

"We need people to stand alongside us and help us fight for our rights, but we also need them to allow us to dictate what we want and need."

In the following viewpoint, Joseph D. Robbins describes his own experience growing up with severe learning disabilities. He notes that many people helped him succeed in school and learn to advocate for himself. Once he had the skills of self-advocacy, he was able to lobby for his own needs and wants in high school and beyond. This helped him achieve success in education and later life. Joseph D. Robbins is the assistant director of the Union for Reform Judaism's Presidential Disabilities Inclusion Initiative.

AS YOU READ, CONSIDER THE FOLLOWING QUESTIONS:
1. What led to the author's success in school, in his view?
2. What is the most important thing people who do not have disabilities can do to help those with disabilities, according to the author?
3. What does "Nothing about us without us" mean?

"Why Self-Advocacy Is Vital to the Pursuit of Disability Rights," by Joseph D. Robbins, Union for Reform Judaism, February 17, 2017. This post originally appeared on ReformJudaism.org and is reprinted with permission from the Union for Reform Judaism.

Whether or not you enlist the aid of an advocate to help you achieve a desired result, it's important to remember that you alone know what's in your best interest.

Like any child, growing up I relied on the support of my parents. Due to my severe learning disabilities, this support was even more essential. Although I was reading at age 4 and showed a propensity toward math, teachers were concerned about me advancing grades in school because of my handwriting—which we later learned was a direct result of my visual motor skills disability.

I went to a Jewish day school that cared deeply about my needs and my education, but as a small school without expertise in the area, was not able to meet these needs. Fortunately, my parents were able to get me the supplemental resources I needed to be able to succeed.

Over the years, I worked with a speech language pathologist, occupational therapists, and a learning specialist, with whom I met multiple times a week from eighth grade through high school grad-

Higher learning institutions are required by law to provide accommodations to students with proven disabilities. Some examples are interpreters or note takers for students with hearing loss, screen reading and voice recognition software for students with severe vision loss, and extended time for testing.

uation. Each of them was committed to enabling me to succeed on my own, and one day, to advocate for myself.

Once, in high school, my guidance counselor refused to let me take an Advanced Placement English course, believing the writing would be too much for me. After lobbying her on my behalf, my parents told me I'd be able to take an Honors English course instead. The next time I was supposed to register for classes, I met with the same guidance counselor and, this time advocating for myself, convinced her to allow me to take five elective English courses—and I received A's in every one.

Come college, I attended the University of Arizona to be a part of the SALT (Strategic Alternative Learning Techniques) Center, the leading comprehensive academic support program for college students who learn differently. SALT allowed me to receive everything I needed academically, while surrounded by students with disabilities. Because SALT employees, as a rule, would not advocate on students' behalf, I gained the confidence to be a self-advocate with my professors and other instructors. By the time I graduated, I was meeting with my learning specialist on an as-needed basis for the first time since middle school, and I'd graduated early with a double-major, a certificate in a third subject, and the merit-based SALT Center Senior Academic Award, awarded to one senior from each graduating class.

I was able to complete both of my graduate degrees with no outside support, lobbying for my accommodations on my own and doing what I needed to make sure my needs were met—and again, I was able to succeed. I received a Masters in the Teaching of English and another in Educational Leadership, and I graduated as part of Kappa

Delta Pi, the national education honors society. These days, I mentor students with disabilities and work with their families, specifically as they navigate the college application process.

As is true for any marginalized group, it's crucial for people with disabilities to have allies. We need people to stand alongside us and help us fight for our rights, but we also need them to allow us to dictate what we want and need. Earlier this year, I attended Jewish Disability Advocacy Day, an annual event that brought nearly 200 Jewish advocates to Washington, DC, to lobby members of Congress on disability-related legislation. For me, one of the most-heartening parts of the day was seeing my fellow disabilities self-advocates, in addition to all of our wonderful allies.

Today, as assistant director of the Union for Reform Judaism's Presidential Disabilities Inclusion Initiative, I work with many people with disabilities, and many people of all abilities who are allies to the disabilities community. Every person I encounter is passionate about the rights of people with disabilities. When I work with people who do not have disabilities but advocate on behalf of those who do, I remind them that the most important thing they can do on behalf of people with disabilities is to listen to our needs. Do not assume what we need; ask us what we need.

One of the overarching mantras of the disabilities self-advocacy community is "Nothing about us without us." It's vital that those of us with disabilities are the ones leading the charge, dictating what we need, and guiding disabilities policy. This is one of the reasons I'm proud to be a part of the Ruderman Family Foundation's Link20 Self-Advocacy Network.

My parents gave me the greatest gift anybody can give a person with a disability: the ability and courage to become a self-advocate. For a long time, I didn't envision myself attending college, let alone attending graduate school and becoming an educator and self-advocate. I'm thankful to my parents for instilling in me the skills and confidence to advocate for myself, for always being an ally to me, and for knowing that the best way they could stand by me was to push me to advocate for my own needs.

EVALUATING THE AUTHOR'S ARGUMENTS:

In this viewpoint, author Joseph D. Robbins supports the idea that people with disabilities should be their own advocates. Compare this article to the previous one. While each made the same point, one used academic research and the other shared personal experience. When would each of these techniques be most useful in convincing readers?

Facts About Self-Advocacy and Disability Rights

Editor's note: These facts can be used in reports to add credibility when making important points or claims.

Terms to Know

- Advocacy refers to the act of supporting a cause or proposal.
- An advocate is someone who argues for or supports a particular cause, policy, person, or group.
- A lay advocate is a paralegal, a person trained in legal matters but not qualified as a lawyer.
- Other advocates may have specialized training, such as in health care or special education. Advocates can also be family members of people with special needs, or people can be their own advocates.
- A disability is a physical or mental condition that limits a person's senses (such as sight or hearing), movements, or activities. Some people have multiple disabilities. In many cases, the limits may be overcome with appropriate aids or services.
- The Disability Services Act of 1993 defines "disability" as meaning a disability:
    - which is attributable to an intellectual, psychiatric, cognitive, neurological, sensory or physical impairment or a combination of those impairments
    - which is permanent or likely to be permanent
    - which may or may not be of a chronic or episodic nature
    - which results in substantially reduced capacity of the person for communication, social interaction, learning or mobility and a need for continuing support services.

Students with Disabilities

- The Individuals with Disabilities Education Act (IDEA) is a federal law passed in 1975. It requires schools to serve the educational needs of eligible students with disabilities. It lists 13 disability categories covered by the law. Schools must find and evaluate students suspected of having disabilities. If disabilities are found, the schools must provide those students with special education designed to meet their individual needs, for free. The school must get parental consent before providing services to the child. The law requires public schools to provide a "free appropriate public education" that is targeted to the student's individual needs. This does not necessarily mean the "best" possible education or the education preferred by the parents.

- According to the National Center for Education Statistics, about 13 percent of all public school students receive special education services. In the 2015-16 school year, 6.7 million students ages 3 to 21 received special education services.

- In education, *integration* refers to including students with special needs in regular classrooms. This is opposed to *segregation*, where the students are placed in special education classes. *Inclusion* also refers to teaching children with and without disabilities in the same classes. A general teacher and a special education teacher may work together with the children. Sometimes the terms integration and inclusion are used interchangeably. Yet there are differences, according to the United Nations Committee on the Rights of Persons with Disabilities. Integration requires the children with disabilities to adjust to the regular classroom requirements. Inclusion involves changing the teaching methods, content, and so forth to overcome barriers. Then all students in the classroom are able to participate equally.

Other Laws Addressing People with Disabilities

- The Americans with Disabilities Act (ADA) is a 1990 law. It prohibits discrimination against people with disabilities. It covers jobs, schools, transportation, and all places that are open to the general public. It is intended to make sure that people with disabilities have the same rights and opportunities as everyone else. The 1990 law was amended in 2008 and faced additional amendments in 2018. The United States Department of Justice Civil Rights Division provides information through a website and phone lines.

- The ADA also addresses postsecondary institutions (colleges, universities, vocational training schools, etc.). These places must provide necessary accommodations when a student discloses a disability. Accommodations provide an alternative way to accomplish the course requirements. They should not make the work easier, but they should reduce barriers related to the disability. The school is not required to provide accommodations until the student has provided evidence of a disability. An example of an accommodation is extended time for testing. Students with hearing loss might get interpreters or note takers. Students with severe vision loss might get screen reading and voice recognition software.

- The ADA gives people ways to enforce their rights if a business is not accessible. They can file a complaint with the US Department of Justice (DOJ). The DOJ will then investigate the alleged violation and decide if the business has violated the ADA. If so, the DOJ may mediate between the individual and the business. Or the DOJ may instead sue the business on the person's behalf. In addition, people with disabilities may file a lawsuit directly.

- The Disability Integration Act (DIA) was introduced in 2017. Its goal is to provide more community-based services to seniors and people with disabilities. This would allow people to receive services in their homes, so they will not be forced into institutions such as nursing homes. As of this writing, the DIA has not been made into law.

- The ADA Education and Reform Act (HR 620) passed the House of Representatives in 2018. Many disability advocates oppose this bill. They believe it will weaken protections given to them under the ADA. HR 620 gives businesses more time to address problems before someone can bring a lawsuit. Those in favor claim it will prevent unnecessary lawsuits from people trying to make money. Disability advocates claim it will allow businesses to avoid complying with the ADA. They claim it weakens civil rights and makes it easier for businesses to discriminate. At the time of this writing, the bill had not been considered by the Senate.

People with Disabilities in the Workforce

- Labor force participation is defined as the people ages 16 to 64 who are currently employed or seeking work. For people without disabilities, 64.5 percent are in the labor force. For people with disabilities, less than 20 percent are in the labor force. A fifth of workers who are not disabled work part time. A third of workers with disabilities work part time. Working part time can mean that people are not working as much as they'd like.
- Health insurance is an issue for people with disabilities seeking work. Many jobs will not fully pay for their healthcare. People with expensive health needs may be better off claiming disability benefits rather than working. Disability benefits are government payments. They are made to people who can't work because of long-term medical conditions.

Organizations to Contact

The editors have compiled the following list of organizations concerned with the issues debated in this book. The descriptions are derived from materials provided by the organizations. All have publications or information available for interested readers. The list was compiled on the date of publication of the present volume; the information provided here may change. Be aware that many organizations take several weeks or longer to respond to inquiries, so allow as much time as possible for the receipt of requested materials.

ADAPT
1208 South Logan Street
Denver, CO 80210
640-A E. 2nd Street, Suite 100
Austin, TX 78702
(512) 442-0252
email: adapt@adapt.org
website: http://adapt.org/
This grass-roots community organizes disability rights activists to engage in nonviolent direct action, including civil disobedience. The goal is to assure the rights of people with disabilities to live in freedom. Download The ADAPT Activist Handbook from the website's Resources page.

Advocating Change Together (ACT)
1821 University Avenue, Suite 306-S
St. Paul, MN 55104
(800) 641-0059
email: act@selfadvocacy.org
website: http://selfadvocacy.org/
A grassroots disability rights organization run by and for people with developmental and other disabilities. ACT furthers the self-advocacy movement by developing new leadership. The group offers workshops, peer networks, and training materials.

American Association of People with Disabilities (AAPD)
2013 H Street, NW, 5th Floor
Washington, DC 20006
(202) 521-4316; (800) 840-8844
website: www.aapd.com/
The American Association of People with Disabilities is a bridge between the disability community and the community at large. Its advocacy programs aim to improve the lives of people with disabilities and increase their political and economic power.

The Arc
25 K Street, NW, Suite 1200,
Washington, DC 20006
(800) 433-5255
contact form: https://www.thearc.org/who-we-are/contact-us
website: www.thearc.org
With almost 700 state and local chapters, The Arc advocates for and serves people with intellectual and developmental disabilities and their families. Chapters offers information, referral services, employment programs, and recreational programs.

Center for Parent Information and Resources
c/o Statewide Parent Advocacy Network (SPAN)
35 Halsey Street, 4th Floor
Newark, NJ 07102
(973) 642-8100
email: malizo@spannj.org
website: www.parentcenterhub.org/
The Center for Parent Information and Resources is a hub of information and products created for Parent Centers serving families of children with disabilities. While primarily directed at parents, the website has a section of Resources for Youth with information on becoming a strong self advocate.

Human Services Research Institute
East Coast Headquarters
2336 Massachusetts Avenue

Cambridge, MA 02140
(617) 876-0426
West Coast Headquarters
7690 SW Mohawk Street, Bldg K.
Tualatin, OR 97062
(503) 924-3783
contact form: https://www.hsri.org/contact
website: www.hsri.org/
Professionals provide research, support and guidance to clients looking to improve service systems for people with disabilities.

Milestones Autism Resources
4853 Galaxy Parkway, Suite A
Warrensville Heights, OH 44128
(216) 464-7600
email: info@milestones.org
website: milestones.org/
Milestones Autism Resources is an online resource center focused on educating and coaching family members of people with autism. The website offers toolkits, a recommended reading list, and a Resource Center. A page on Self Advocacy and Self-Determination lists appropriate advocacy skills for each age and offers additional resources (http://milestones.org/individuals-with-asd/self-advocacy/).

National Alliance on Mental Illness (NAMI)
3803 N Fairfax Drive, Suite 100
Arlington, VA 22203
(703) 524-7600
contact page: https://www.nami.org/Contact-Us
website: https://www.nami.org/
The National Alliance on Mental Illness is a grassroots mental health organization dedicating to building better lives for those affected by mental illness. The group offers educational programs, a helpline, and public awareness events and activities. It also helps shape public policy relating to mental illness.

National Disability Rights Network
820 1st Street NE, Suite 740
Washington, DC 20002
(202) 408-9514
TTY: (220) 408-9521
email: info@ndrn.org
website: http://www.ndrn.org/
A nonprofit organization dedicated to improving the lives of people with disabilities. The group advocates for laws protecting civil and human rights. Public policy addresses education, employment, health care, and more.

For Further Reading

Books

Douglas, Deb. *The Power of Self-Advocacy for Gifted Learners: Teaching the Four Essential Steps to Success (Grades 5–12)*. Minneapolis, MN: Free Spirit Publishing, 2017.

A resource for helping gifted teenagers advocate for their needs in education.

Hayes, Amy. *Disability Rights Movement (Civic Participation: Fighting for Rights)*. New York: PowerKids Press, 2017.

Photographs and primary sources bring the disabilities rights movement to life, highlighting key figures and events.

Iriarte, Edurne García, and Roy McConkey. *Disability and Human Rights: Global Perspectives*. Basingstoke, UK: Palgrave Macmillan, 2015.

This book draws on international research and real-life examples to explore disability as a global issue.

Meeks, Lisa. *Parties, Dorms and Social Norms: A Crash Course in Safe Living for Young Adults on the Autism Spectrum*. London, UK: Jessica Kingsley Publishers, 2016.

A guide for young adults on the autism spectrum. This book covers topics such as relationships, sex, drinking, emotional health, and independent living.

Paradiz, Valerie. *The Integrated Self-Advocacy ISA Curriculum: A Program for Emerging Self-Advocates with Autism Spectrum and Other Conditions (Student Workbook)*. Shawnee, KS: Autism Asperger Publishing Co, 2009.

A curriculum that teaches self advocacy, especially designed for people on the autism spectrum.

Sandbox Learning. *Time to Stand Up for Myself! How to Become a Self-Advocate (Teen Topics)*. Charlotte, NC: Sandbox Learning, 2012.

This book is designed to help teenagers with disabilities stand up for themselves and advocate for their goals. It includes strategies for problem solving, communicating, and finding support.

Shapiro, Joseph P. *No Pity: People with Disabilities Forging a New Civil Rights Movement.* New York: Broadway Books, 2011.

A history of the disability rights movement and how it led to the Americans with Disabilities Act.

Shogren, Karrie A., PhD, and Paul Wehman, PhD. *Self-Determination and Transition Planning (The Brookes Transition to Adulthood Series).* Baltimore, MD: Paul H Brookes Pub Co, 2013.

A book designed for educators to teach students skills they need to successfully enter adulthood. Young people may benefit from the worksheets and activities.

Tuttle, Cheryl Gerson, and JoAnn Augeri Silva. *Self-Advocacy: The Ultimate Teen Guide (It Happened to Me).* Lanham, MD: Scarecrow Press, 2007.

This book offers teenagers tools to help them advocate for themselves, with real world examples

Periodicals and Internet Sources

"Basic Advocacy Skills," School Advocacy Hamilton. http://www.schooladvocacy.ca/basic%20advocacy.pdf.

Block, Lydia S., "Self-Advocacy in Educational Settings," LD OnLine. http://www.ldonline.org/article/Self-Advocacy_in_Educational_Settings.

Buzaglo, Joanne, "Empowering Patients to Become Effective Self-Advocates," November 17, 2016. https://www.psychologytoday.com/blog/the-patient-s-voice/201611/empowering-patients-become-effective-self-advocates.

"How to Be an Advocate for Yourself and Others," The Well Project, June 30, 2016. http://www.thewellproject.org/hiv-information/how-be-advocate-yourself-and-others.

James, Nancy Suzanne, "Self-Advocacy: Know Yourself, What You Need & How to Get It," Wright's Law. http://www.wrightslaw.com/info/sec504.selfadvo.ld.nsjames.htm.

Lucio, Antonio, "The Importance of Self Advocacy," Huffington Post, December 13, 2011. https://www.huffingtonpost.com/antonio -lucio/the-importance-of-self-ad_b_1147035.html.

Magnuson, Eric J., and Lisa L. Beane, "Oral Argument—Learn by Listening," Robins Kaplan, September 10, 2015. http://www .robinskaplan.com/resources/articles/briefly-oral-argument -learn-by-listening.

Pola-Money, Gina, "Self-Advocacy," Medical Home Portal, 2014. https://www.medicalhomeportal.org/living-with-child /navigating-transitions-with-your-child/transition-to-adulthood /self-advocacy.

Preeta, "Role of Lawyers in the Legal System," iPleaders Intelligent Legal Solutions, October 1, 2011. https://blog.ipleaders.in/role-of -lawyers-in-the-legal-system.

"Professional Advocacy Services Principles and Standards," Family Rights Group, 2009. https://www.frg.org.uk/images/PDFS /advocacy-standards.pdf.

"Self-Advocacy: A Valuable Skill for Your Teenager with LD," Great Schools, October 14, 2016. https://www.greatschools.org/gk /articles/self-advocacy-teenager-with-ld/.

"Self-Advocacy: Empowering Individuals with Disabilities," Special Needs Planning, August 27, 2015. http://specialneedsplanning .net/2015/08/self-advocacy-empowering-individuals-with -disabilities/#.

"Self-Advocacy and Personal Futures Planning," Connecticut State Department of Education: Bureau of Special Education Transition Task Force. http://www.ct.gov/brs/lib/brs/pdfs/guidepostdocs /SELFAdvocacyAndPersonalFuturePlanning.pdf.

"Self Advocacy in Higher Education," National Federation of the Blind. https://nfb.org/self-advocacy-higher-education.

"Tips for Being an Effective Advocate," New Brunswick Association for Community Living. https://nbacl.nb.ca/module-pages/tips-for -being-an-effective-advocate/.

"What Is Self-Advocacy?" Heartland Health Advocacy Resource Network, 2014. http://heartlandselfadvocacy.org/what-is-self -advocacy/.

Websites
Kids as Self Advocates (KASA) (www.fvkasa.org)
A grassroots project created by youth with disabilities for youth. The website offers resources such as advice on going to college, online dating, staying safe, and much more. Members can join a forum or share poetry and artwork in an online "Café."

Self Advocates Becoming Empowered (www.sabeusa.org)
SABE's mission is "To ensure that people with disabilities are treated as equals and that they are given the same decisions, choices, rights, responsibilities, and chances to speak up to empower themselves; opportunities to make new friends, and to learn from their mistakes." The website offers newsletters and information on becoming a member.

Wrightslaw (www.wrightslaw.com)
A website for parents, educators, advocates, and attorneys, Wrightslaw provides information about special education law and advocacy for children with disabilities. While primarily directed at adults helping children, the Self Advocacy page at www.wrightslaw.com/info/self.advocacy.htm has many resources. Sign up for the free, weekly Special Ed Advocate newsletter.

Youthhood (www.youthhood.org/index.asp)
A website for teens that offers advice on preparing for life. Sections focus on high school, jobs, community, health, living independently, and knowing your rights.

Index

Picture Credits

Cover Lisa S./Shutterstock.com; p. 11 J.D.S/Shutterstock.com; p. 14 Amelie-Benoist/BSIP/Corbis Documentary/Getty Images; p. 22 wavebreakmedia/Shutterstock.com; p. 27 iMoved Studio/ Shutterstock.com; p. 33 Alex Wong/Getty Images; p. 37 John Lee/ First Light/Getty Images; p. 39 michaeljung/Shutterstock.com; p. 47 Marcel Jancovic/Shutterstock.com; p. 52 Scott S. Warren/National Geographic Magazines/Getty Images; p. 57 iofoto/Shutterstock.com; p. 64 Molly Riley/Reuters/Newscom; p. 69 Andersen Ross/Blend Images/Getty Images; p. 71 Elnur/Shutterstock.com; p. 78 goodluz/ Shutterstock.com; p. 87 Milwaukee Journal Sentinel/Tribune News Service/Getty Images; p. 94 Blend Images - Andersen Ross/ Brand X Pictures/Getty Images; p. 101 Monkey Business Images/ Shutterstock.com